RECLAIM YOUR THOUGHTS

CONQUER NEGATIVE SELF TALK AND NEGATIVE THINKING BY USING PROVEN PRACTICAL TECHNIQUES TO IMPROVE YOUR EMOTIONAL INTELLIGENCE

DR. STRONG D.C. DACNB, CFMP, PAK

© **Copyright 2020 - All rights reserved.**

The content contained within this book may not be reproduced, duplicated, or transmitted without direct written permission from the author or the publisher.

Under no circumstances will any blame or legal responsibility be held against the publisher, or author, for any damages, reparation, or monetary loss due to the information contained within this book, either directly or indirectly.

Legal Notice:

This book is copyright protected. It is only for personal use. You cannot amend, distribute, sell, use, quote, or paraphrase any part, or the content within this book, without the consent of the author or publisher.

Disclaimer:

Please note the information contained within this document is for educational and entertainment purposes only. All effort has been executed to present accurate, up to date, reliable, complete information. No warranties of any kind are declared or implied. Readers acknowledge that the author is not engaged in the rendering of legal, financial, medical, or professional advice. The content within this book has been derived from various sources. Please consult a licensed professional before attempting any techniques outlined in this book.

By reading this document, the reader agrees that under no circumstances is the author responsible for any losses, direct or indirect, that are incurred as a result of the use of the information contained within this document, including, but not limited to, errors, omissions, or inaccuracies.

CONTENTS

Introduction — 7

1. What did you say?! — 15
2. Know the Stakes — 42
3. Pinning Down Your Demons — 61
4. How did I get here? Where did it start? — 76
5. Dethroning the Tyrant — 94
6. From Tyrant to Friend — 105
7. The Cultivation of Kindness — 134
8. A Bright Future — 147

References — 163

"The happiest and most successful amongst us know the deep difference between being alone and being lonely"

SPECIAL BONUS!

Want These Bonus Affirmations and A Case Study for FREE?

Get FREE, unlimited access to these and all of our new books by joining our community!

Scan w/ your camera To JOIN!

INTRODUCTION

"You're terrible! No really, you are! Have you ever just listened to yourself – I mean, really listened, closely, as if your life depended on it?

The truth is, that your life DOES depend on it - the quiet internal abuse you seem to dish out to yourself is far worse than all the sorrow the world could muster – don't waste your life!! Please, do yourself a favor, do the world a favor, and learn how to treat yourself with care, love, and compassion"

First and foremost, I want to take a brief moment to thank you personally for embarking on this journey inside my mind. The concepts in this book come from my own personal experience, as well as the hundreds of patients I have worked with over the years. Normally, in my other books, I include a testimonial from one of my patients' successes but this book is different. I hold this topic dear to my heart and would like to share my own testimonial. Are you ready?

My story of negative self talk began around the age of eleven. Why might you ask? At this age, I had become overweight, wore braces, glasses and was unathletic. Definitely not what you would consider a "cool kid" back then or in today's world. Nearly two hundred pounds as an eleven year old, it was a challenging time of my life, especially in transitioning to my teenage years. Thoughts of low self-worth and self esteem plagued my mind almost every second of every day.

These encompassing thoughts prevented me from engaging with my peers, attending events and developing emotional stability. Over the next eighteen years, I struggled to rid myself of these thoughts which were hindering my development and growth. Even in my twenties, this emotional turmoil from my younger years, engrained certain behavioral patterns. No longer was I an overweight eleven year old but a decently well developed man. However, I could not disassociate with the ghost of my past. My mind still envisioned myself as that eleven year old boy and this is how I thought the world saw me as well. Seeing myself in this light greatly restricted my social engagement and ability to push myself. Part of me contemplates how different or more successful I would have been without these thoughts holding me back.

After many years of studying, self development and working with others, I have come to understand the complexity of the human mind. The inner workings of a vastly complex matrix that makes us who we are. Can we control our mind, thoughts or reactions? Are we subjected to the consequences of our environment, teachings or fate with no control? My argument is that you can make the choice, now, today to take back those thoughts and control them just as I have. So, reclaim your thoughts using the techniques in this book. Become the person you want to be without self-doubt, negative thinking or self loathing. Make the choice NOW but enough about me. Let's begin your journey.

Your life does depend on how you talk to yourself. The way that little voice talks to you inside your head represents the way you think and feel about yourself. This is especially true if you have an oppressive negative tyrant inside that berates you, judges you, undermines your activities, and makes you feel worthless for every perceived mistake.

The voice inside your head can be positive, compassionate, encouraging, critical, and insightful. But many of us develop an extremely negative inner voice that completely dominates our inner world and affects our perceptions and emotional states.

Imagine having to live with an inner voice that constantly spews forth toxic streams of negativity, judgment, and self-doubt every single hour of your day. Eventually, drinking from that toxic river of thought will poison everything you do. Such a voice can erode your confidence, lead to depression, cut you off from taking good opportunities, and prevent your plans from succeeding.

Time to wake up!

If you have a negative inner voice that constantly undermines you and diminishes you then it is high time to dethrone this inner tyrant and take back your own personal sovereignty!

That is what this book is all about. It describes typical patterns of negative self-talk and negative thinking, and then it will show you how to identify those negative patterns, stop them in their tracks, and then it shows you how to actually *transform* your inner critical voice into something that serves you for a change.

Learn how to create inner distance from that voice, and learn simple and powerful strategies to eliminate the negativity that constantly spews forth within you.

In the end, if you want to start liberating yourself, you need to learn how to get out of your own way and start to bring some positivity and skillfulness into your inner states.

Everything starts to flow when you get your own house in order. Part of getting that house in order is to look after your health, drop what doesn't serve you, take a systematic approach to heal the voice within, and then sealing the deal by making sure that the inner tyrant never comes back to abuse and harm you ever again.

This book introduces you to a systematic, step-by-step approach to gradually create the kind of positive and radiant inner conditions necessary to have a happy and successful life. Life may still throw you lemons, but you will be vastly better prepared to make the necessary lemonade if you become your own best friend.

No one would willingly abuse themselves. Nobody would volunteer to sabotage their own happiness and success. Yet that is exactly what people do; over and over again they repeat the same negative habitual patterns of behavior without realizing that they have been the architects of their own misery.

Nine times out of ten it is that inner negative critical voice that contributes to self-defeating patterns of behavior. The behavior is irrational and subconscious and often automatic (no one would consciously choose to do it), but that doesn't mean you can't do anything about it; YOU CAN!

This book is a comprehensive workbook that will take you step-by-step from simple beginnings where you begin to notice what you are doing, to dramatically ambitious (but easily accomplished once you know how) efforts that will leave transform your inner voice into your best friend that serves you. Free yourself from your past negative conditioning, it no longer serves you anymore. Taking the journey ahead in this book could be one of the most empowering and satisfying choices you will have ever made for yourself.

I know it works, I've had to take the journey myself. As a functional medicine doctor and chiropractic neurologist, I have had the pleasant opportunity to share these methods with my patients. They're extremely effective, simple, and they work.

Now I am happy to have the opportunity to share those same methods with you.

I know you probably won't believe me now, but you ARE deserving of the things you want in your life. You CAN achieve your goals, and you aren't alone. Let this book be one of the few companions that have, up till now, actually supported your goals and happiness. Then watch as your life unfolds in new and exciting directions free of the harrowing negative chains of a toxic inner critic. The journey starts in chapter 1, begin there, and watch everything fall into place.

1

WHAT DID YOU SAY?!

WHAT IS SELF-TALK?

To put it most simply, self-talk is what we say to ourselves. People sometimes vocalize their self-talk out loud, but by far the majority of self-talk that happens in people takes place inside their heads, privately. When I talk about "self-talk" throughout this book I always mean both kinds - word-thoughts and vocalizations. They have equal importance since they both reveal a lot about what we think of ourselves and what we think of the world in which we live.

This personal inner monologue can be positive or negative; and it always combines conscious thoughts with unconscious beliefs about ourselves and the events and circumstances of the world we find ourselves in.

As we shall see in more detail in later sections of this book, positive self-talk can be really beneficial in several important ways like supporting the health of the body, keeping motivated, reducing depression, helping us to achieve life goals, calming our fears, and boosting our motivation and confidence.

Negative Self-Talk (NST) also has effects on our well-being too, negative effects. We'll get into these more deeply in later sections too. Inappropriate self-critical self-talk is unfortunately a part of human nature. Too often such negative talk can convince people not to try (and hence fail right out of the gate). Saying things like, "I can't", or "I'm a failure", or "I don't deserve XYZ" are classic examples of a self-defeating critical inner voice and we will learn how to undo these kinds of negative self-talk habits later on.

There is a difference between self-reflection and negative self-talk. Some people find their negative self-talk motivating in that it galvanizes them and motivates them to do better. But, the truth is that negative self-talk is not constructive by definition. In the long run, it will harm people's confidence.

On the other hand, Self-reflection is a much more constructive activity because it is the act of looking honestly and *consciously* at one's behavior and beliefs and questioning those beliefs *to improve one's being and station in life.*

This is completely different from negative critical self-banter which is almost always completely unconscious and does not look to identify weak points as sources of opportunity for positive change and growth. Critical negative self-talk might motivate some people in the short term, but in the long run, it can never lead to sustained benefit because is never looks for solutions or positive adaptation – ultimately negative patterns of thinking serve to undermine a person's happiness, and it doesn't motivate us to make positive changes and grow as people. This book will encourage you to be self-reflective, but it will never encourage you to engage in negative self-talk and thinking. [1]

For now, it is helpful to realize that the way we speak to ourselves matters because there are very real consequences to viewing ourselves overly critically, as opposed to being our own best friend.

Your inner monologue gives your brain a way to interpret and process your daily experiences – the narrative you hold with yourself will be based on your conscious thoughts in combination with your unconscious beliefs, biases, and assumptions. If you listen carefully enough, and you know what to look for, you may discover that your inner monologue can be very revealing of your own nature and tendencies. Becoming conscious of your inner dialogue is the very first step you will need to take to undo negative self-talk habits and then go on to engineer a positive relationship with yourself and your self-conversation habits.

Without being aware of your own negative self-talk you will not be able to catch yourself 'in the act' of being self-defeating. That is what I would like to tackle first in this chapter – the different kinds of NST so that you will recognize them and begin to notice it clearly when you discover it within you. If you notice it and know what type of NST habits you are guilty of doing, then you can learn effective strategies to undo your negative habits. Before we get to practical solutions, we do need a map of the terrain. For the remainder of the chapter, I'll describe the different kinds of negative self-talk in brief detail. [2]

TYPES OF NEGATIVE SELF-TALK

According to the literature, there are four main kinds of self-talk category and many other less commonly occurring ones. The four main ones are known as, "Personalizing", "Catastrophizing", "Filtering", and "Polarizing" types of negative self-talk.

Each type or category of negative self-talk is usually labeled according to its characteristic pattern of negativity, or style. [3] In addition to the four most common categories of negative self-talk, there are actually many other slightly different forms of negative self-talk that happen in many people, albeit less common than the main four categories.

In the next section, I will explore these four main types of negative self-talk and then I'll describe all the rest of them too so that you can begin to cultivate your own inner awareness of when they arise in you.

To recognize negative self-talk it is very helpful to know your inner psychological terrain beforehand - and having some labels and tools to help identify different kinds of negative self-talk within you is the perfect first step to recognizing your inner psychological terrain. [4]

THE FOUR MAIN CATEGORIES OF NEGATIVE SELF-TALK

Personalizing

"It's not you, it's me"

Taking responsibility for things in your life is usually considered a good thing, especially when you recognize that you have done some objective factual wrong. However, taking appropriate responsibility is quite different from inappropriately taking things personally based on your thinking. What is meant by "personalizing" negative self-talk here is the act of unrealistically taking responsibility for negative outcomes in an excessively way.

What happens in people who have an excessive inappropriate sense of personalization is that they blame themselves for being the cause of every little bad thing that happens to them or someone else. The reason this is a poor habit to have is that in most cases your assessment that it was *solely* your fault is often completely factually incorrect – just plain false. Most situations in life are complex and multifactorial. Most bad things that happen to people happen due to a combination of factors they could have controlled in combination with many factors completely out of their control. For people who have the negative habit of over personalizing, they tend to ignore all the other factors that were not under their control in favor of beating up their own self-image and placing the blame squarely on their own shoulders.

A classic example includes having a big blow-out argument with a friend and then deciding that you were the one to blame and apologizing, even when the blame should be shared.

Another classic example of personalized overthinking is when a friend or partner chooses not to spend time with you by declining a date or event plan. Most healthy and well-adjusted people cultivate healthy friendships and they know that their friends care for them. For the person who does not overly personalize events or behavior, they don't take the decline personally; as if it were a judgment of their quality and value as a person. But, in people who compulsively talk to themselves negatively by overly personalizing people's behavior around them, this can feel like a hurtful rejection – the reason why they did/said XYZ is because, "I'm just not amazing enough", "it's my fault", "I'm a terrible person" and so on.

Another good example is when you text your group of friends in a group- chat on social media and your friends take much longer to reply than they normally would. If you start thinking, "Oh, they must be angry with me"; "they don't like me"; "they don't want to be friends anymore...", then you would be guilty of over personalizing their slow response time.

99 times out of 100 the slow response time will have absolutely nothing to do with you at all, and if you didn't take tiny things so personally, you wouldn't feel so bad about yourself – typically people are busy, enjoying their own lives and not really thinking of you at all; which is good, healthy, and normal. When they get to it they'll respond, but their tardiness will have nothing to do with who you are as a person, especially if you really are friends.

Imagine being at a party and overhearing a conversation between your friends who are sitting in the next room. Imagine they are complaining about someone, sharing negative events, and things about that person. People who over personalize are almost always going to assume that they are being talked about in this situation, even when there is no good evidence pointing to the fact that the subject of the conversation is you. People who have the unconscious negative habit of over-personalizing events and situations and behavior *fear that the reason why things happen is because of how horrible or worthless they think they are.* This is the classic characteristic of over-personalizing self-talk and it is very bad for your self-esteem because it distorts the way you interpret life situations.

A quick Tip: First Steps to Reduce Overly Personalized Negative Self-talk

To begin to deal with these kinds of social over-personalizing self-talk you will need to be aware of your inner feelings and thoughts, catch them as they arise – that is the first crucial step that must be taken to deal with any type of NST.

Once you notice that you are over-personalizing, then you can pause, after which you could ask yourself a few well-placed questions like, "Is this true?"; "Do I know, for sure, that the reason why they are doing XYZ is because of something about me?"; "Am I really to blame?".

This beginning strategic tip is actually a form of 'reality test' because it forces you to stop your negative thought processes and start being critical by measuring your automatic negative assumptions against what you actually know about the present situation. It is a process of 'checking in' to reality and the hard objective facts.

Even though you might still feel emotionally fearful that your negative self-thoughts are true, the process of challenging those thoughts, paying attention to reality, recognizing what you actually factually know, and then evaluating the truth of those negative thoughts can actually interrupt personalization in its tracks. This is because engaging the critical thinking areas of the brain tends to move your brain activity away from the emotion and fear centers to the prefrontal cortex (the part of the brain responsible for planning and abstract reasoning). Doing some critical internal thought inquiry actually changes the way your brain functions and can lead to a massive reduction in anxiety – which helps to see the situation with clarity and objectivity; it also interrupts the stream of negative thinking too.

Some of the questions you could consider asking include:

- Is there any evidence supporting the thought that I am somehow to blame, responsible, or a bad person?

- Did the negative thoughts about myself come from facts right here right now, or am I interpreting events negatively without knowing the full facts?
- What alternative explanations could combat my interpretation? Why assume the worst when I could assume something more positive instead and feel great about who I am and how my friends and acquaintances see me?

Reality testing and challenging your thoughts and assumptions in the moments that they arise takes a bit of practice. You will need to be aware of what you're thinking and feeling in the moment to catch it and interrogate your mind consciously. Don't worry if you don't catch it the first ten times, keep reminding yourself to be vigilant, and then you will catch yourself indulging in negative over personalization at some point. Once you catch it even once, it won't be as hard to catch it the next time – gradually you can eliminate this nasty form of self-deprecation and enjoy friends, family, and social gatherings without much of the stress and anxiety that often comes with poor negative self-talk in these situations.

Catastrophizing

"I am doomed – the little things told me so"

Catastrophizing is when we let minor mishaps in our day completely ruin our inner emotional states. Often people assume the worst outcomes and then become angry, despondent, sad, demotivated, or depressed as a result. People with this negative habit often become defeated and pessimistic about future outcomes just based on something tiny not going as expected.

Some people say that we should, "expect the worst", because then, "…you won't be disappointed by people or life".

I can't tell you how many people have said this very thing to me throughout my life, and almost always these people tend to be grumpy, unhappy, diminished, and emotionally impoverished shadows of who they could be.[5]

A good example of catastrophizing is when you get stuck in traffic and assume it will take the maximum time for you to get to work or home. Assuming the worst about being stuck in traffic then leads to assuming the worst about the rest of your day.

A person who catastrophizes tends to emphasize extreme negative future consequences based on present events – unreasonably so. They do not entertain the most likely outcomes, nor do they fantasize as much about positive outcomes as they do about negative ones – they focus only on the worst ones. It's like thinking that the world will end after you spill some coffee on your shirt while driving – it is a negative pattern of anticipation in response to something small going poorly.

Why would anyone assume the worst will happen? There are very few situations where 'assuming the worst' is actually a good practice. An example of "assuming the worst" that makes sense and adds value might be in the case of engineering and designing public infrastructure. In that case, one has to assume the worst and put conservative safety margins to counteract potential catastrophic failure. To do this, engineers must assume that failure is inevitable, and then do everything they can to reasonably limit disaster in those situations.

The above kind of prudent planning based on 'what could go wrong' is completely appropriate when planning a space rocket trip, or safety margins for elevators, or an isolated hike in the mountains. It is constructive and beneficial and prudent. Catastrophizing on the other hand seldom comes with a constructive and appropriate effort to prepare for future outcomes.

Speaking generally, catastrophic thinking as a form of prudent preparedness only makes sense when catastrophe is a realistic consideration. Catastrophizing NST is not like this, it is an *inappropriate* response to a small cue or event that leads to negative mental and emotional states.

In everyday situations, catastrophizing is based on inappropriate and unreasonable assumptions about future outcomes – an overreaction to some small event that spells disaster for the rest of the day. If you realize that this is what is happening then you could ask yourself why do I choose to assume the worst would happen when it would be just as reasonable to assume the best outcomes? Most people would answer that avoiding disaster is worth anticipating, even when it doesn't happen.

Unfortunately, people tend to catastrophize because the human brain evolved to be very good at it. Catastrophizing is an important evolutionary advantage because it helps us recognize that the rustling in the bushes next to us on the path could be a dangerous predator, so we should run and save ourselves. This means that we always survive, even when we are wrong. That is why catastrophizing is hard-wired into our brains, humans have gained an evolutionary advantage from being able to anticipate danger and avoid it – at the cost of avoiding a 'danger' that wasn't really present in the first place.

In people with toxic habits of self-talk who constantly catastrophize every little thing, they tend to have way too much anxiety and hopelessness about the future than is healthy, they may also begin to believe that they will always be victimized by the next situation…

If you always think the worst is going to happen, then you will likely avoid taking simple risks, and you will tend to exaggerate situations and events in your life as being very negative when they simply aren't at all. This puts you in a state of chronic tension, anxiety, and stress, which can really impact your physical and mental health over time, not to mention prevent you from taking the amazing opportunities that life constantly throws your way. On the other hand, people who feel that life is abundant and supportive, and filled with challenge and opportunity tend to be more successful and fulfilled – they also tend to see themselves in a much more dynamic and powerful way, one where they actually do have a decisive say in the events that happen in their own lives.

Feeling like you have agency and opportunity in your life goes a long way to feeling good about your life and your achievements, and can have a positive effect on your daily motivation and happiness. By preventing catastrophizing negative self-talk you won't unrealistically feel the dramatic victim of life's unforeseen circumstances.

If you detect catastrophic self-talk within you, then you can challenge those thoughts and really ask yourself "how likely is it that? Really, how likely is it that these terrible outcomes will definitely happen?". Instead of feeling like the worst is definitely going to happen, you can be open and ready for what actually does happen. You can allow life to surprise you with how supportive it can actually be; how abundance can flow into your life if only you give it a chance to enter.

Try to consider how likely your assumed catastrophes actually are. Try to consider other outcomes instead; more reasonable expectations based on your real past experience, not your fears about the worst-case scenario. Being stuck in traffic, being paid late, people not calling you, not getting that job, not having good luck, these things might not mean the 'end of the world', in fact, they usually don't mean that, far from it.

Catastrophes are extreme and are usually very unlikely – we shouldn't really be expecting them to happen very much at all unless your job is to plan for them explicitly. However, 'slightly uncomfortable mini-challenges' are in fact quite common, and not such a big deal if you aren't disconsolate and demotivated because you assumed the worst.

The trick is to be mindful enough to catch this habit and nip it in the bud because unreasonable catastrophizing is harmful to your sense of self-worth, power, and personal feelings of agency. Even if the worst does happen, won't you be alright in the long run? Usually, the answer to this is, "yes", if you realize that fact at the moment it can be a big relief. Taking a step back and checking in with reality can really help keep your stress down, which will help you make clearer decisions and meet the world head-on.

Negative Filtering

"I only notice the truth – the negative truth of course because I'm such a realist!"

Filtering, as the name implies, just means filtering out (ignoring) most positive aspects of a situation, person, or event, in favor of a biased lopsided view; viz. your own negative view.

Catastrophizing is really a form of filtering, as is personalization, as are all the other types of negative self-talk. The reason this is the case is that to believe the unreasonable and repetitive negative self-talk, we have to ignore crucial facts about ourselves and the world; positive facts. We could not really believe our own NST whilst facing the truth of the world.

That being said, negative self-talk is a learned conditioned habit of mind which we have fallen into - it is not rational behavior at all. Most of us know that it isn't rational, the irrationality of NST is not really the issue, the habit of doing it is the issue; and it can be very difficult to break.

Catastrophizing the future is different from describing the present negatively while ignoring all the positive aspects of the present. Filtering is about not paying attention to the positive aspects of the present moment and emphasizing and paying attention to the negative aspects.[6] An every-day example of filtering is when you have a goal to save X amount of money per month and you manage to only save 90% of your target amount. Instead of being proud of managing to save 90% of your target amount you focus on that missing 10%. People who are guilty of filtering might even judge themselves as useless, as not being able to achieve their own goals or fulfilling their own promises. Judging yourself for going over budget completely ignores (filters out) the fact that you did manage to save a significant sum of money in the first place – which could be cause for some pride in oneself.

Filtering is choosing to see the glass as half empty, lacking, missing half of what is needed. Filtering means that you approach things negatively instead of recognizing the objective fact that the negative aspects might only be a tiny fraction of the whole truth.

Thinking that contextualizes events negatively is just the same as framing the glass as half empty instead of half full. Positively framed (half full) thinking is beneficial and contributes to longevity, better health, sustained motivation, and better psychological outcomes. 'Half-empty' thinking that frames situations and events past or present negatively have been shown time and again to be self-defeating, biologically harmful, and psychologically damaging.

People who negatively filter their assessments of situations and things tend to judge their 'failures' as more important than their little successes. The truth is that most major achievements are accomplished in small daily increments (little daily 'wins'), not one massive effort. Recognizing that the small 'wins' guarantee the big one's help you to realize that your efforts really matter – setting your sights on the daily tasks at hand helps you to see the true value of what you are doing day to day, rather than judging yourself when you fall short of unrealistic expectations.[7]

People who negatively filter obsess over their imperfections, or their perceived 'failures' – they are often perfectionists. If you find yourself filtering, or feeling like nothing is going right, or devaluing yourself because you couldn't manage to reach your lofty ideals, then it can help a lot to remind yourself of all the things that have actually gone right recently.

Bring back to conscious awareness all those things that you filter out and your tendency to become discouraged or feel like a failure becomes less and less each day because you gather the correct *perspective and* context for the events and situations in your life. Writing down the things that have gone right for you recently is a good way to attack this negative tendency head-on.

Polarizing Self-Talk

"All or nothing, black or white – angel or demon"

"Polarizing" is sometimes called "all-or-nothing" thinking, or "black-and-white" thinking. With polarizing, you see things only as either good or bad. There is no middle ground. It's the feeling that you have to be perfect otherwise you're terrible, or that other people are either all good or all bad, or that life has to go perfectly right down to the little things.

A classic example would be when you get up early and get productive every day. Then, one morning you're a bit tired and you sleep in. If you suddenly feel like you are a lazy failure then you would be guilty of polarizing negative self-talk.

Polarized thinking is quite similar to negative filtering because to be completely good you have to ignore all the bad and vice versa – the same truth applies when we judge other people in a polarizing fashion to be either all good or bad. It is helpful to have compassion for yourself and others and forgive the trespasses and give yourself a break from overly criticizing yourself when you don't live up to your own standards. No one is completely perfectly a saint or a sinner; we're all just humans with good points and bad points, good days, and bad days. The normal state of affairs is to recognize your own humanity, love that, and be kind to yourself when you break your own inner code – it is going to happen from time to time.

A good quote that sums up [8] If you don't do something perfectly, reassure yourself that you're only human. You're allowed to make choices that cater to your needs at the moment. And sometimes, what we view as a mistake can become a lesson or motivation to keep trying.

Mind Reading

"They hate me; they're bored; they don't want to be around me..."

Mind reading happens whenever we think we know what others are thinking or feeling without any real evidence – we assume their inner mental and emotional states without any good evidence to support our assumptions.

Mind reading is negative when we imagine that other people's actions are motivated by negative attitudes towards ourselves. Some examples may make this clearer:

Imagine giving a presentation at school or work and some people in the audience seem distracted or yawning, playing with their phones, or staring out the window. If you assume that they are distracted because your speech is bad, or they don't like you, or some other reason that paints you in a negative light then that would be assuming without much evidence that you were somehow inadequate. This is mind-reading because you assume you know WHY they are doing what they are doing and it paints you in a negative light.

Imagine another scenario where you arrive home and your girlfriend or wife doesn't greet you or hug you hello right away. If you start believing and thinking that she is upset, perhaps upset with you for some reason, then that is again negative mind reading – there could be many reasons for her behavior. Perhaps she was just tired and distracted after a long difficult day at work herself?

Overgeneralization

"I will never be able to...because this one time..."

Overgeneralization is when we expect negative circumstances in the present to keep happening over and over again in the future. It is a form of exaggerating negatively. For example, imagine you apply for a job and your application is rejected. If you then say to yourself, "I'll never get a job, see, I didn't even get this one!" then you assume that the specific negative case happening right now will keep happening – "why even bother applying for jobs anymore, I'll just get turned down".

A similar scenario often happens to people when they attempt to ask someone out on a romantic date...if rejection leads you to conclude that you will never find a romantic partner, then you have over-generalized this one failure. The same can be said for ordering food at a restaurant and it arrives cold, "I always get the worst luck at restaurants!"

Magnification

"I can't remember names at a party....that proves my memory is bad...now I don't even try, what's the point? My memory is bad..."

Magnification is exaggerating your own flaws or errors. This can be a bit like catastrophizing because we can take small personal problems or qualities or events and blow them out of proportion by thinking they lead to disastrous outcomes.

The theme for magnifying is "taking a small mistake and thinking that the worst happens because of it. Some great examples of this include

- Mistaking someone's name in a meeting or at a dinner party, and then thinking that they will judge you as selfish; or that you aren't interested in other people.
- You feel mild pain in your lung and then completely worry you have lung cancer or some other terrible disease and need to rush to get medical treatment (similar to catastrophizing)

Minimization

"You think I did great, but actually, I should have done better, just look at this little mistake, obviously I'm not so great!"

This is the opposite of magnification and happens when you ignore, minimize, or deny your positive qualities completely. This prevents you from taking pride in your own strengths and can land you in a negative cycle of feeling inferior and worthless. Good examples of minimizing include:

- You cook an amazing meal, but you obsess over the fact that the rice was ever so slightly overcooked – making you think the meal was terrible, or that you could have done better.
- You play an amazing tennis match and win after a titanic struggle on the tennis court, but you criticize yourself because you should have done better.

Emotional reasoning

"You're a horrible person every time I have a bad day"

Using emotions in the present moment as a guide to what you decide to do can lead people to avoid discomfort and unpleasant emotional states. This can lead to procrastination and depression. People who exert effort and experience some discomfort in the pursuit of their most cherished goals tend to have a deep sense of fulfillment but people who orient their actions based on emotional reasoning will tend to avoid making that effort because it is unpleasant in the immediate moment. Some examples include:

- I'm not going to go to do my maths homework today; I really don't feel up to it.
- If I was more motivated I would enjoy my training, but I'm not, so I'm not going to train.

Fortune telling

"Why does the worst always happen to me?"

Fortune Telling is like overgeneralization because it involves predicting a negative outcome in the future based on what happened in the present – except that in both cases there isn't much evidence to support our conclusion. Overgeneralization is more exaggerated than fortune telling which is usually contained to the outcome of a specific event. Good examples include:

- After writing an exam we assume we did poorly even when we aren't sure.
- After going to a job interview you assume that they didn't like you because you were 'mind-reading' and

then you 'tell your fortune' by saying there's no way you got the job because they clearly didn't like you.

Labeling

"You're a bad person!"

Labeling is when people apply a negative descriptive label to a person or event in an extreme way. A classic example of this is calling someone a bad person because they were rude to others in a public place. The truth is people are complex and always changing, they could have just been having an 'off' day. Usually, people are a mix of multiple characteristics that cannot be described by a single simple conceptual label that forever brands them as a certain type. Labeling can be done to others or to the self and is a form of polarizing thinking – a negative oversimplification of the truth.

- You have a fight with your best friend of 20 years and then label that friend as an obnoxious jerk.
- You do poorly on a test at university because you were stressed and then you think to yourself that you're an unintelligent idiot because you can't get a good grade.

Should statements

Using the word should, particularly in hindsight, can be very self-judgmental and pressurizing. Life is impossible to predict and in any one moment, the key factors at play are almost infinite, making it difficult to know what the best course of action should be.

In hindsight, it is much easier to judge ourselves as being stupid for what we have done or did not do, but this does not acknowledge the context of that moment. Ambiguity, uncertainty, and inherent risk are all part and parcel of real-life situations. Reflecting on past actions and learning from them is a positive and constructive attitude to take; judging yourself as being incompetent and idiotic is not constructive.

Putting ourselves under pressure in the present moment to always find the right course of action, the 'should' at any moment, puts us under pressure to be perfectly adapted in every situation. Clearly, this kind of negative judgemental pressure cannot be helpful and indeed can lead to anxiety, poor self-worth, and a habit of being hyper-critical post hoc.

The other thing such an approach may lead to is a paralyzing inability to be proactive and decisive since based on past judgments which were based on a 'should ' mentality - people may fear doing the wrong thing.

Saying "should" places immense pressure on yourself to perform in the present moment. While this might motivate you on occasion, if you place yourself under this kind of pressure all the time and then judge yourself for falling short of your own (perhaps unreasonable) expectations then this kind of thinking can only lead to resentment, anxiety, and stress.

- If a friend drops by for a visit and you don't have food in the house to offer him because you haven't gone shopping yet. Then if you believe you are a "bad friend", or a "bad host", because you should have anticipated the company and been prepared.

You feel you must always keep the house absolutely clean and spotless for yourself (and especially for guests) but an old friend drops by and you feel like a lazy failure when it comes to managing a home environment.

2

KNOW THE STAKES

This chapter is all about the damaging consequences of engaging in the destructive habit of talking to yourself negatively (negative self-talk; NST). The classic school playground saying, "sticks and stones will break my bones, but words will never harm me!" turns out to be false – or, at least not entirely true.

Words are not physical 'things', they are literally symbolic representations of things, beliefs, and concepts. What this childhood saying seems to imply is that words, as representations of real things, aren't physical objects, so they could never be the sort of thing that causes any physical harm like breaking bones. But, this statement is actually false in two important ways.

Firstly, NST is definitely linked to changes in your body which impact your physical health. A good example of this fact is that a study done on negative thinking showed that it causes high blood pressure, even when not currently having any negative thoughts.[1] High blood pressure is linked to a whole variety of dangerous and debilitating chronic diseases, not least of which is a major risk factor for the number one killer disease of the modern era, heart disease.

Secondly, physical harm is not the only kind of harm either, we can and do suffer psychological wounds that can affect our moods, emotions, thought processes, perceptions, motivation, sense of self-worth, and life choices extremely negatively.

In this chapter I many of the most commonly reported consequences of NST that crop up in the scientific literature. Understanding the danger of continuing to engage in the destructive and self-defeating habit of talking to yourself negatively will ultimately help you to realize that what you say to yourself matters; significantly so.

Although some of the damaging effects I describe in this chapter might be surprising to some who might have underestimated the damaging effect words can have on health and well-being, the truth is that it isn't that surprising on an intuitive level once you think about it. Imagine that you have a friend that always criticized you and put you down and deliberately deceived you about your opportunities and value as a person – eventually you wouldn't want to spend time with that 'friend' because you would realize that you always feel bad after hanging out together. But, this is what happens with people who engage in the habit of NST. Essentially, when you engage in chronic NST you become your own worst friend, and there is no way to spend time away from yourself. Constantly letting your inner best friend put you down and tell you that you're never good enough will wear away at your mental and physical health – closing the door on that negative inner friend should become a priority because constant day and night critique will eventually come to erode your quality of life in every domain.

The danger of constantly engaging with NST is that it becomes a habitual way of relating to yourself, others, and the world around you. If it becomes habitual and unconscious, you could be harming yourself every single day and not realize it! Naturally, it is the constant and unrelenting nature of the inner critic which doesn't ever give you a break which will lead to horrible consequences. Intuitively most people can feel that the consequences of being the victim of such a toxic inner dialogue would be far-reaching, gradual, and dangerous. Once the behavior is entrenched as an unconscious habitual tendency, then it can be extremely hard to notice, let alone extinguish. NST is such a habit that requires awareness and moment-by-moment mindfulness to eliminate – this takes time and diligence, you won't extinguish the negative talk all in one day. That's why it is important to stay motivated and to realize what is at stake if you don't keep up with combating this dangerous behavior. That is why this chapter is very important – you need to know the dangers so that you can recognize them in your life and keep motivated day-by-day and eliminate every behavior that no longer serves your greatest benefit.[2]

THE CONSEQUENCES OF NEGATIVE SELF-TALK

Balanced self-criticism is a normal part of balanced healthy thinking patterns, and it definitely has survival value. However, when self-criticism becomes an endless habitual cycle of negative self-talk, it can distort the very way you perceive people and events in your life. NST is a pathological habit that completely fails to give people a true reflection of themselves or their circumstances. NST is completely unlike the positive habit of constructive self-critique which always aims to review one's behavior with the idea of growing and improving one's lot in life.[3]

Limited thinking

NST can lead to narrow and poor thinking that results in a reduced ability to anticipate and capitalize on opportunities. A tendency to blame oneself when things go wrong has been shown to contribute to feelings of failure, and depressed mood. Highly self-critical people also often feel guilty and ashamed when something goes wrong – they dump the perceived fault inappropriately on their own heads.[4]

Doing this on a chronic daily basis definitely leads to a serious erosion of confidence and also reduces your ability to think clearly, which is why it impacts people's ability to see opportunities or capitalize on them successfully. The more you tell yourself you can't do something, the more you believe it, and the more you end up being paralyzed in action – unable to respond decisively to life's events.

Ultimately, NST can perpetuate a feedback cycle of downward spiraling negative life choices and outcomes which lead to even more negative self-talk, anxiety, poor health, and many other unpleasant states of mind. If you end up believing your inner hyper-critical voice the consequences can be especially dire in the long term, this is supported heavily in the research literature – one study found that self-blame over negative events is linked to an increased risk of mental health problems.[5,6]

Perfectionism

NST often gradually escalates thinking that results in people being afraid of being associated with something less than perfect. In fact, research has indicated that self-critical tendencies are linked with perfectionism, self-harm, and eating and food issues.[7] Aside from body image, eating and food issues, perfectionism is a serious problem for people with habitual NST.

The assumption is that perfection is realistic and achievable. But, unfortunately for people with a habit of NST, their self-talk always makes it much more difficult for them to evaluate things as perfect! This is a particularly vicious trap that commonly affects people with certain kinds of NST habits.

In general, 'high achievers' end up doing better than perfectionists because they navigate their lives with far less stress – they do not have to wrestle with the negative mental and physical health consequences of chronic stress that arises from putting themselves under pressure to perform at a 'perfect' level.

Sometimes It is true that "Done is better than perfect". A job well done IS perfect, no need to pressure oneself to attain unrealistic ideals of perfection that simply cannot be met in a reasonable and sustainably healthy way. This implies that people who are high achievers (but not perfectionists) do not overly ruminate and try to pick out every single little flaw to make something great into something perfect. They are happy with excellence – which is healthy and balanced and serves the world perfectly. Unfortunately for people with NST, there is often no middle ground, it is either 'perfect' or nothing at all because NST is often polarizing and extreme in nature.

Feelings of depression

There is quite a lot of research literature showing that negative self-talk leads to increased feelings of depression, irritation, aggression, demotivation, anxiety, and perceptual distortions.[8] In fact, studies show that if NST is left unchecked for too long it ends up being extremely psychologically damaging.[9][10][11]

Relationship Challenges

NST can severely impact interpersonal relationships. NST often contributes to others perceiving you as needy or insecure. In addition to that, NST can 'generalize' into behavior that is generally antisocial and negative which may bother others putting a strain on personal and work relationship dynamics.[12][13]

Feelings of loneliness and isolation are common to people plagued with habitual patterns of NST. Loneliness and isolation can actually contribute to a person's withdrawal from others and make it more difficult to assert personal needs and desires. People with NST who also go on to exhibit avoidant behavior are also more likely to be submissive in relationships with others, usually out of a fear that asserting their own needs and opinions will lead to even more criticism than they give themselves.[14]

There is no mistaking the link between NST and challenging effects on interpersonal relationships. For example, a study done in 2005 showed that low self-esteem (common in people with NST) relates to higher risks of physical and verbal aggression toward others.[15]

OTHER CONSEQUENCES OF NST

There are in fact a whole host of reported consequences of NST in the literature. One study done in 2009 at Bangor University in the United Kingdom (specifically in Wales) reported positive, negative, and neutral consequences of NST. The study highlighted the fact that more than 50% of all consequences of NST were negative and harmful to individuals' performance outcomes - even when positive consequences were also experienced.

This shows that the power of the negative consequences of NST can undermine the few positive results that might accrue from being hyper-self-critical. The negative consequences of NST that were reported in this study included: [16]

- Reduced performance (slow pace of activity, stopping activity, and poor actual performance of activity)
- Reduced motivation to continue with tasks
- Negative emotional consequences
- *Feeling negative emotions like discontent, stress, anger, frustration, annoyance, and embarrassment.*
- Decreased Psychological control
- *Loss of focus or ability to concentrate*
- *Decreased mental performance*
- *Increased pressure on self to perform*
- *Poor decision making*
- Negative mental processes and cognitions
- *Imagining one's own future actions in a negative way (negative fantasies of future performance)*
- *Negative self-perception (Feelings of being useless and/or worthless)*
- *Self-doubt (Uncertainty in one's ability to complete challenges or achieve milestones)*
- *Decreased mental resilience and increased negative perceptions of body states (feeling tired more quickly, overestimating negative body feedback like little aches, pains, or fatigue)*

NST Prevents All the Benefits of Positive Self-Talk

The above points are all negative consequences of NST, but there are also several possible positive and neutral consequences that came out of studies. Some of these positive and neutral consequences may include: [17]

- Triggering self-analysis - (neutral)
- Mixed emotional responses that are neither positive nor negative towards self. – (Neutral)
- Improved performance – (Positive)
- Improved effort – (positive)
- Increased motivation - (positive)
- Feeling more positive about one's self and better moods – (positive)

It might sound strange that NST can be linked to positive outcomes, but for a small minority of people this seems to be the case. It is as if the negative critical voice in their heads keeps them doggedly focused on improving themselves and urging them to do more. Unfortunately, positive and neutral consequences to NST tend to be experienced by a tiny minority of people, and even if positive consequences are experienced they tend to be undermined in the long run because of the gradual insidious nature of NST and the accumulation of negative effects on thinking, perceptions, and body health. The negatives definitely outweigh the positives because they eliminate all the benefits you might receive. [18]

On a slightly different note, and relevant to the heading for this small section is the fact that one of the most obvious drawbacks of negative self-talk is that it isn't positive self-talk. This sounds obvious, but the point is important to make because research has shown that *positive* self-talk has many remarkable benefits – positive self-talk is a very good predictor of success.[19]

A study was done on athletes that compared four different types of self-talk (instructional, motivational, positive, and negative) found that *positive self-talk was the greatest predictor of success.*[20]

This means that people who engage in NST habits will miss out on all the benefits of positive self-talk habits.

THE BIOLOGY & PSYCHOLOGY OF SELF-TALK; CYCLES WITHIN CYCLES

Self-talk, both positive and negative, result in changes in our emotional and cognitive states which can persist over time – particularly if either kind of self-talk behavior is habitual and engaged in over a long period.

One thing you could ask yourself is, "How do these emotional and mental changes come about just from self-talking habits?"

This is a very good question because it asks us to go a little bit deeper into science explaining the underlying mechanisms linked to positive and negative self-talk.

The subject of brain chemistry and physiology, emotions, thinking, and cognition is an extremely complex one. The field is usually studied by neuroscientists and cognitive psychologists along with allied disciplines like biochemistry and medicine. My aim here is not to prepare you for university graduate level exams but to gently describe the most important elements of science's current understanding of the brain-behavior-body connection.

What are emotions, biologically speaking? Everyone can talk casually about feeling happy, or sad, or excited, or fearful, but how do biologists and neuroscientists talk about the emotions. Academic professionals usually talk about emotions in terms of their correlated bio-chemicals. What scientists have discovered by doing investigations into the biology of people experiencing different mental and emotional states is that chemically speaking our subjective emotions are correlated with tiny little messenger molecules called "neurotransmitters".

Neurotransmitters are tiny little messenger molecules that help nerves to transmit a signal to each other. The nerve activity within your brain can be controlled and regulated chemically via the relative concentrations of different neurotransmitters between neurons.

In fact, one of the super-star researchers in the field (she discovered the existence of a site on cells called the 'opiate receptor'), wrote a book in 1999 that was titled "Molecules of Emotion" - a seminal public work that focused on how neurotransmitters and their balance in the body were responsible for different emotional states.[21]

The presence of the little molecules implies that whenever your mood or emotions change, then your biology is also changing in synch with those moods. This also means that if NST induces negative emotional states of being and impoverished cognitive functioning, then it must also be affecting the chemistry of your brain too – in real-time.

A property of the brain is that whenever neurons talk to each other, they fire off signals in networks of interconnections. This works a lot like the internet does, because the internet is a network of interconnected computers that fire off information packets between each other. The brain operates and processes information by firing off informational messages along with networks of interconnected nerves. These networks are called neural networks (a term that has also been adopted into computer programming jargon).

It turns out that people aren't born with all their networks ready-made, they learn and build their nerve inter connections through their habitual behavior and life experiences. Nerves that constantly fire together tend to wire together more strongly. This means that whatever you habitually do tends to become more and more entrenched in your brain's physical structure, organization, and chemistry. Our habits lead to gradually learning new skills, and eventual mastery of those skills.

Unfortunately, the ability of the brain to form stronger neural networks by repeating specific behaviors also applies to your NST habits. The more that people engage with NST, the more the brain builds a network of neurons together for those habits. This means that the little neurotransmitters associated with your NST are also increased – leading to a greater ability to experience negative emotional states, stress chemicals, and poor health outcomes from these changes.

This means that unhealthy habitual NST tends to reinforce itself as behavior, and eventually leads to pathological emotional states and poor cognitive functioning in addition to all the other effects I have written about above.

To put it simply, NST involves the reinforcement and building of neural networks that get increasingly better at undermining the confidence and health of people. In point form, the details can be very broadly summarized below: [22]

NST...

(Promotes negative moods and impacts our organs and systems' functioning via many feedback loops)

1. NST (combined with stress) increases the release of stress chemicals called catecholamines (hormones released by the adrenal glands).
2. Catecholamines as stress chemicals act as 'neuromodulators' in the central nervous system (affect neurotransmitters and nerve function) and as hormones in the blood.
3. Catecholamines rise when there is a perceived danger, but they are also significantly increased by engaging in negative self-talk, as is the most important stress hormone of all, cortisol.
4. High levels of cortisol have many damaging health effects especially if they remain elevated over long periods – something that will happen in people who engage in NST. Specifically speaking, chronically high cortisol levels can shrink the volume of the left prefrontal cortex, which is the part of the brain associated with positive emotions.
5. This means that chronic NST has strong and significant negative physical and mental consequences.
6. It turns out that circulating hormones and

neurotransmitters engage in a feedback loop that impacts overall health, weight management, digestion, mood, motivation, and drive – something that is driven and perpetuated by NST.

The discussion so far has been about the basic science of negative self-talk and how it leads to chronic cycles of ever-increasing negative consequences for the body and mind. The discussion so far has also pointed out that NST leads to more and more NST, so it is very important to break the cycle as soon as possible to prevent the most serious buildup of debilitating attitudes, health, and emotions. But what about positive self-talk? It turns out that exactly the same mechanisms are involved with positive self-talk, except that the molecules involved are different. The neurotransmitters might be different for NST as they are for positive self-talk, but the mechanisms of neural nets and feedback cycles remain pretty much the same. In the case of positive self-talk, people not only prevent engaging with negative self-talk and all those negative consequences but actually generate upward cycling feedback loops of ever-increasing benefit!

Two neurotransmitters (called "GABA" and "serotonin") are linked to positive self-talk. They are both responsible for calming the body and mind as well as supporting satisfaction and feelings of fulfillment. In other words, GABA and Serotonin can keep anxiety in check – leading to feelings of self-worth, increasing happiness, and protecting against depression and demotivation.

Other important neurotransmitters are also implicated in positive self-talk. Dopamine is linked to pleasure and feeling rewarded and oxytocin is linked to feeling love and affection and bonding – particularly in long term relationships. Dopamine promotes motivation, interest, and drive in addition to pleasure - it keeps us from feeling meaningless and 'grey'.

I hope that it is clear that these hormones and neurotransmitters are directly impacted by our thoughts and internal conversations. The scientific research keeps showing the relationship between behavior and these molecules of emotion. So, it stands to reason that making an effort to maintain positive thoughts and self-talk will have vast and varied benefits to the basic biological structure of your body as well as improve your subjective emotional and mental states.

OTHER NOTABLE STUDIES SHOWING THE RELATIONSHIP BETWEEN BODY AND MIND

A 2013 study done by researchers at Florida State University College of Medicine discovered that teenagers in the study with completely normal weight profiles who *thought* (mistakenly) that they were overweight were much more likely to become obese later in life.[23]

A study done on negative thinking in the 1980s showed what happens when college students reflect on the negative outcomes of recent stressful life events as opposed to reflecting on the positive outcomes.[24] The students who focused mainly on negative outcomes were measured as having lower self-esteem, lower reported levels of personal satisfaction, and were much more likely to be experiencing psychological trauma eight weeks after the event.[25]

The researchers went on to speculate that negative thinking might prevent individuals from mentally healing, recovering, and moving on from traumatic life events; "…[negative self-talk] results in ongoing emotional distress and spontaneous mental intrusions [linked to the event]…"[26]

It seems that the research indicates that focusing on the negative aspects of a life event makes it far more likely to keep replaying the traumatic event over and over in the mind's eye and for longer periods too. This keeps inducing emotional distress in the present moment. Repeated and repetitive negative thinking patterns tend to constantly affect people's emotions and perceptions negatively making it harder to think clearly and navigate life's daily challenges; as well as making it much more likely to describe challenging situations as traumatic whilst also making it more and more difficult to resiliently overcome such situations and move on with life in a healthy unburdened way.[27]

As this chapter draws to a close I would like to emphasize that it is important to recognize that the way you speak to yourself has a significant effect on your emotional states, your mental performance, and the health of your physical body. Engaging in chronic and habitual negative self-talk will create feedback loops in your psychology, biology, and life circumstances that lead to repeated frustration, social alienation and discomfort, poor health, and failure to achieve one's personal goals and preferences. In short, NST as a habit needs to be nipped in the bud as soon as you can manage to do it – there is simply too much at stake not to.

3

PINNING DOWN YOUR DEMONS

In chapter 1 I described different types or categories of negative self-talk. Each category of negative self-talk has harmful consequences for both body and mind which is something we covered in detail in chapter 2. Now in Chapter 3, it's time to begin answering the question, "what can I do to eliminate the harmful habit of negative self-talk from my life completely. The rest of this book is dedicated to exploring the best ways to eliminate negative self-talk from your life so that you can begin to cultivate the mental space to support your deepest wishes for your life.

The best way to eliminate the harmful habit of negative self-talk will vary slightly from person to person. Each person comes with a unique set of circumstances, past history, cultural conditioning, and beliefs and assumptions. This means that each person will probably have their own unique set of NST categories within them. Even though there are naturally going to be differences in the kinds of NST people have there are a few universally applicable factors that would apply to anyone who is looking to develop and implement a strategic plan to combat their inner critical demons.

The first requirement to working with your inner voice when it is negative is to be aware of it, and then recognize it when it happens. I have mentioned this fact before in both chapter 1 and chapter 2, and I am repeating and emphasizing it again here because it is arguably the single most important ability to have to even begin to transform your inner monologues into something positive.

If you aren't even aware of your own negative self-talk when it happens then it will be impossible to do anything about it. This means that cultivating a certain watchful inner vigilance is necessary to begin reforming your inner narrative. You will need to cultivate a kind of mindfulness of your inner voice, emotions, and thoughts so that you become a witness and watcher to your inner world while you go about your daily activities.

However, watchful witnessing and mindfulness of your inner psychological states are not sufficient on its own to change your habitual tendencies, but it will enable you to bring your unconscious habitual inner critic into the light of your conscious awareness. This will enable you to see, recognize, and identify your own particular forms of NST. Once that is achieved and you can catch yourself in the moments you are beginning to engage in NST, then you can employ an effective strategy to counteract the particular flavor of your NST – whether it be a compulsive habit of personalization or a tendency to catastrophic reactivity to minor events.

How do you develop a witnessing awareness and vigilant attention? The first steps to doing this are to revisit the descriptions of each kind of NST that I described in chapter 1 and write down which ones apply to you. Then begin to watch your mind and emotions for small moments repeated many times throughout the day, whenever you remember. In the beginning, you won't catch yourself engaging in your negative self-talk with much success, but if you stick with it and remain determined to catch yourself doing it you will eventually catch it as it is happening. When you manage to catch yourself for the first time you can congratulate yourself on making meaningful progress. Then from there, you will begin to slowly catch yourself a little more often. With practice, you will eventually be able to catch yourself more often than not, and then you will have turned a corner in transforming your inner critic into someone who actually supports your dreams and goals and improves your life.

So, the first step is to be aware of your internal states, notice what is going on, practice as much as you can remember, and keep at it – your brain will learn to do it and get better at it with time because you will develop a healthy 'self-aware' neural network that works to guard your inner self for the better.

If you train your mental attention and vigilance you might want to investigate basic meditation techniques to get a little daily practice while sitting calmly and comfortably. This is helpful, especially in the beginning, because it can be difficult for people to retain awareness of their inner mental states while they are doing other things at the same time. Watching your body, speech, and mind is much easier when you are sitting quietly and calmly on a cushion compared to keeping your awareness while talking on the telephone or paying for your groceries.

Perhaps the hardest contexts for people to remain aware of their inner voice during busy daily activities are those where you find yourself distracted, focused, or challenged by competing stimuli – places like a dinner party, social gathering, your busy workplace, in the car stuck in traffic. These situations can all be quite distracting and triggering - they might present a bit of a challenge at first. Don't worry about it, with a bit of practice you'll get the hang of pointing your mind inwardly whilst doing things outwardly – like anything worthwhile, it just takes a bit of consistent practice.

Once you have had some practice at remaining vigilant and aware, you will eventually be in a position to witness your own negative self-talk taking place in real-time – instead of remembering back and catching it after the fact. The very first step is bringing your behavior out of the realm of the unconscious and into the realm of the conscious. But, what you might find at this point is that even though you can catch yourself most times you engage in negative self-talk, and even though you can recognize the kind of negative self-talk that you are prone to engage with, that does not mean you know what to do about it. Knowing what to do about your NST in the present moment requires a few helpful learnable strategies that you can easily implement. After becoming aware of your NST, the next step is to recognize it or label it for what it is. After you identify it you can then interrupt your critical thought stream in specific beneficial ways to stop the habit from playing itself out.

You know from reading chapter 1 and chapter 2 that your negative self-talk is detrimental to your happiness and health. You also know that the behavior is quite irrational, usually based on false assumptions or biased conditioning. But, knowing that your behavior isn't rational or healthy is usually not the problem. Most people know that their inner self-talk is not constructive and toxic at some level. The main problem is that the behavior is usually unconscious and that it is resistant to being extinguished. Identifying your inner demons is the first step after cultivating inner mindfulness. This is the topic of this chapter along with tips to help you identify when you might be doing it - It is the start of your practical journey to cultivating a supportive and insightful inner voice of your own.

IDENTIFYING YOUR OWN NEGATIVE SELF-TALK

Think back to the types of negative self-talk outlined in Chapter 1, and remind yourself of the different types of NST that most often plague you. Knowing what you are looking for is very helpful when you are training to catch yourself doing it. Because the behavior is automatic, an unconscious habit, you could stand to benefit from a few tips and hints to help you to spot it in yourself.

One simple yet powerful tip that can help you identify when you're engaging in negative self-talk is to watch for the warning signs that usually arise when you engage with negative thinking.

PAY ATTENTION TO THE COMMON WARNING SIGNS OF NEGATIVE SELF-TALK

Negative self-talk often comes with a few tell-tale characteristics. It is good to be aware of the most common signs so that you can be on the lookout for them when they might happen in you. If you find anyone of these warning signs in your inner mental conversations, then chances are you are engaging in NST.

Short & Snappy!

Inner NST can often arise as short, sharp, snappy, and spontaneous negative judgmental talk. Good examples can include:

- "You look terrible!"
- "Oh, NO!"
- "ugh, I'm such an idiot"
- "What a jerk!"

NST often tends to be quick and spontaneous and automatic. Usually, there is some negative judgment attached to or contained in the words. Not all snappy statements inside your head will be negative, but many will be.

Expanded Words

A lot of the most common forms of NST include words that express overgeneralizations or absolutes that ignore the reality that not everything is always bad. If you catch your inner voice using these absolute words or making extreme overgeneralized statements then check-in to see if there is a negative self-judgment or not.

Absolutes or exaggerated overgeneralizations often include words like:

- Always (I'm always forgetting things)

- Never (I'll never find a romantic partner)

- Everybody/nobody (Nobody loves me, everybody hates me)

- Everyone/No one (everyone thinks I'm a fool/no one likes me)

- Anything / Everything (I can't do anything/everything is so frustrating today!)

Should and Shouldn't

Very often your inner critical demon will attempt to induce guilt within you making you feel like you ought to have done something differently/better. This kind of guilt-inducing language typically uses the words "should", "shouldn't", "must/must not", and "ought". Good examples of this kind of NST include:

- I should have done that differently
- I shouldn't have been so negative!

One simple trick you can use to eliminate the guilt-inducing and pressurizing nature of these kinds of inner thoughts is to ban your use of the word "should". Just simply delete this word from your vocabulary and things will probably go a lot better. If you do need to express a concept that implies a strong urge to some corrective action, then you can substitute the word "could" for "should".

For example,

- "I should have done that differently"
- ---becomes---> "I COULD have done that differently"
- "I must do well in the next exam"
- ---becomes --> "I might be able to do well! Here's hoping"

Notice that using "could" instead of "should" emphasizes freedom of choice and alternative options. Rewriting the over guilt-inducing pressurizing statements of your self-talk with the word 'could' tends to be more compassionate and understanding and allows you to recognize that you could do better next time. Opening up possibilities for yourself with your inner dialogue is much more constructive than narrow demands to get things perfectly right.

Automatically Accepting Irrational Thoughts

Many instances of NST are completely irrational. They tend not to be grounded in factual reasonable reality. The problem is that through habit we might tend to accept them without any critique. If you manage to create some distance within yourself from your inner voice by training your mental awareness and vigilance, then you'll be able to see your thoughts, understand them, and reflect upon whether they are reasonable and rational. This is often far better than just immediately accepting them as a kind of habit.

Great examples of these kinds of thoughts often happen when people catastrophize, over-personalize, or overgeneralize.

- You spill your coffee on your shirt at work, and now "my whole day is ruined, I'll never be allowed to keep working here because I can't even keep my shirt clean" (irrational catastrophizing)
- Overhearing a small part of your friends' conversation you say to yourself, "I knew it, my friends hate me" (over-personalization)

- No one ever listens to me, I'm so boring (irrational overgeneralization in response to negative mind reading and personalization)
- Oh no I forgot my friend's birthday, now they'll hate me forever! (irrational and catastrophic overgeneralization)

Automatic Chains of thought leading to Catastrophe

Sometimes a rapid series or chain of thoughts and images arrive in sequence, one after another. Ultimately these automatic and rapid thought-chains can culminate in disaster. A not uncommon example that affects quite a few people who are prone to catastrophic thinking is when they forget to take their antibiotics and then they imagine extreme negative consequences like getting septicemia and then ending up dead as a result of a small mistake or event. Forgetting to take your pills is not likely to lead to death or a catastrophic emergency. Thought chains of this type can often come with rapid-fire imagery. Very often we get extremely stressed if we just automatically believe the end results to be likely and rational. Heart rate can increase, fear and panic may arise too. Anxiety attacks are commonly induced by catastrophic negative thought chains.

Speaking to your conditioned fears and unrealistic standards

NST Often relates to your irrational conditioned fears and unrealistic standards. For example, if you hold yourself to be the perfect host and fear that somehow you will fail your guests then your self-talk can run automatic chains of embarrassment or perceived failure as you imagine burning the food you're making for your dinner party. Or perhaps you keep judging yourself and what you are saying to your guests because you fear being a boring host, or rude.

Overreacting based on emotional dysregulation or reasoning

Perhaps you've been feeling like you are always treated unfairly, that you get less than the rest because you don't deserve more. This might be the subject of some of your internal NST. Then suddenly you explode angrily in the kitchen when someone uses your warm kettle water for themselves and you escalate a verbal fight into a shouting match with tears and drama for everyone concerned. Clearly, someone using the water you had plans for is only really a mild inconvenience. How would they have known? But, because you have been talking negatively to yourself about being unfairly treated you are sensitive about this topic – highly 'charged' on the issue – so you blow up at a close family member over nothing. Or perhaps you begin to say judgmental things about that family member to yourself in your head based on negative emotions you are feeling that are completely unrelated to them or the present moment and its circumstances.

Very often our habitual NST can engender discontent, aggression, and 'grumpiness' just under the surface, bubbling and boiling and threatening to burst out at just the right little stimulus. Generally, this kind of thinking is automatic, subconscious, overly emotional, and related to one's personal standards.

Saying Things to yourself that you wouldn't dare Say to a Friend

Sometimes our inner voice or self-talk can take on hostile aggressive tones aimed at ourselves. The golden rule is that if you talk to yourself in a way you would never talk to your friends or loved ones then it is likely you are being disrespectful and negative towards yourself.

CREATE SOME DISTANCE FROM YOUR OWN NST TO SEE IT MORE CLEARLY

Practice recognizing NST in Other People

While we are getting accustomed to our own negative self-talk behaviors it can sometimes be difficult to see ourselves clearly because, in a way, we are very self-invested and 'close' to ourselves. It is hard to see clearly when we are too close to something. Therefore many psychologists suggest trying to practice recognizing negative self-talk by listening carefully to others and identifying when they are doing it. This works because there is a little distance between you and your friend's internal dialogue.

In fact, a little distance and separation from one's own negative dialogue can actually really help you to combat the negative consequences of your self-dialogue. If you can detect, and then identify your own NST, then you will be able to place some distance between you and your negative dialogues. This 'distance' can be very beneficial and is actually able to reduce the power of your negative self-talk even before you do anything else.

Thinking about your personal self-talk as it is happening is completely different from simply engaging in self-talk and automatically accepting it as true and letting it run your thoughts and emotions. Practicing with other people is a great way to train yourself to get better at detecting and recognizing your NST habits. Then you can distance yourself from those thoughts just by observing and thinking about them. Another trick is to look out for it in other people - sometimes it's easier to identify examples of negative self-talk in others before we're able to do it for ourselves.

Keep a journal

This is a fantastic way to create a bit of distance between yourself and your NST habits. You might not be able to detect the fact that your thoughts have been automatic and irrational and negative while you are having them. But, hours later, if sit down quietly and mentally go through your day and the events and emotions and thoughts that had throughout the day, you will probably be able to see when your thoughts were negative and irrational and when you were simply flowing from one experience to the next. Keeping a journal helps you to create distance, get in the habit of being self-reflective, and allows you to see repeating patterns in your thoughts and inner dialogue that only appear over time.

Keeping a journal can really help bring your NST up from the 'automatic and unconscious' into conscious awareness. Writing down everything you 'catch' can help you to detach and create the distance you need to see your inner critic clearly and disarm it completely.

4

HOW DID I GET HERE? WHERE DID IT START?

THE COMMON CAUSES OF YOUR NEGATIVE SELF-TALK

Our habit of negative self-talk (NST) is not something that forms suddenly all in one moment. Like most behavioral habits or tendencies, NST is most likely to be acquired or 'learned' behavior. Typically people who engage in NST have internalized a critical voice or attitude and then that attitude gets reinforced such that it becomes an entrenched aspect of their inner personality structure. Although there is not much written directly on the origins of negative self-talk in the academic research literature there is quite a lot of literature that speculates intelligently on how we might first begin to form our critical voice by the time we are five years of age.

While it is true for many people that the inner negative critical voice begins in early childhood, it can actually develop at any time in life for any number of reasons. In this chapter, I want to explore different potential causes of developing a pathologically critical inner voice, from childhood personality factors through to common bad habits and everyday factors that can crop up for many people in their adult lives.

One thing that most experienced experts would probably agree on about NST and what causes it to develop in the first place is that it usually starts in response to some person or negative event in our life and then evolves gradually until a pattern of entrenched inner critical dialogue becomes an unbalanced feature of our adult personalities.

Childhood Psychological Development & Causes of NST

Freud described the human psyche as having three distinct 'parts' or features, the 'Id', the 'ego', and the 'superego'. The id is the part of our psyche that is responsible for our base animal-like drives, desires, and wish-fulfilments – it operates largely unconsciously and impulsively, like an untamed child that constantly has impulsive wants, desires, and needs that have to be fulfilled immediately. The id is that part of us that wants immediate gratification and pleasure and if it does not get what it wants it can throw an angry tantrum, become violent, or sulk and withdraw and become passive-aggressive.

The id is the home of our most raw and primal base animal instincts and if left unchecked would dominate human adults by making them completely impulsive in a socially inappropriately way. The id is violent, sexual, pleasure-seeking, vulnerable, and lacking any idea of appropriate social conduct or rules. The strategy of the id is to simply take what it wants without regard for others and satisfy itself at any cost.

Have you ever felt a deep craving for chocolate such that it drives you to turn your car around and go into the store to buy one – that's your id pushing itself and its needs into your consciousness. The same can be said of fantastical thoughts of violence towards others you might be angry with. The id can often bubble up to its reactions to thwarted desires in fantasy and imagery which might even be disturbing or extreme. For example, if you happen to have an argument with your best friend and then suddenly you have a mental image of murdering your friend (!) then you can be sure your id, your primal animal instinct, is bubbling up to consciousness. Freud hypothesized that we all have this primal force inside our psyche and that other parts of the psyche split and develop to manage and mediate these primal forces.

The second part of the psyche to develop is the ego, which is like a mediator or negotiator between the undaunted bottom-up urges of the id and the top-down instructions of the super-ego. The ego is the filtering device that takes inputs from other parts of the psyche and brings them to fruition in reality. The ego is our sense of agency and self and it is our interface with reality. The ego learns to be prudent because it learns to strategies on behalf of the id in such a way as to promote success and cohesion. As an analogy, if a horserider is an 'ego', the horse would be the primal powerful force of the 'id' that pulls and pushes us in different directions, the ego drives the horse, but not by itself, it uses the reigns (the 'super-ego') to keep the horse pointing in the right direction and holding back the wild inner desires and fears of the 'id'.

The super-ego is the part of the psyche to develop last out of the three, and Freud speculated that it develops by about age five. The super-ego is the part of our psyche that has internalized social and moral codes of conduct. The super-ego is like our inner parent as a lawgiver, and its function is sometimes to be critical. The superego hands down restrictions and critique to crush the id, the ego tends to mediate between the tension between the id and super-ego. Freud claimed that what characterizes the human psyche is the psychological tensions that arise from the interactions between the three parts of our psyche. According to Freud, if all three parts of our psyche are in a healthy balance, then people will have a healthy integrated personality structure and be resilient, positive, and healthy from a psychological perspective.

But what does all this have to do with your negative self-talk? If you think about Freud's theoretical model of the psyche carefully you might recognize which part is likely to be responsible for your negative hyper-critical inner voice – your super-ego.

If you look at your personality structure from a Freudian perspective then that constantly negative internal critical dialogue that runs inside you is a manifestation of an imbalanced psyche that has an overly dominant hyper-critical super-ego structure that is crushing the id and ego under the weight of its standards, moral codes, restrictions and ideals of perfectionism.

How does the super-ego develop? Typically it is the internalized voice of our early parents during the formative years of very young childhood. If we had overly critical parents or caregivers that constantly lambasted us for our actions and explorations during childhood then that hyper-critical parental voice can often become internalized and made 'our own'. From then on we have to live with a monstrous inner critical demon that constantly questions and undermines the efforts of the ego and id to bring forth their energy in a healthy and balanced way.

Our early childhood experiences can often affect our basic underlying assumptions about the world. If some traumatic childhood event befalls a child or a family then people may internalize that "the world is not safe". In cases of childhood abuse, whether physical, direct emotional abuse, or indirect abuse like neglect, children can often internalize that they are basically worthless, that the world is hostile, or that if they don't act properly they might end up dead, hurt, and in pain.

In a sense, the way we talk to our children indeed becomes their inner voice; their super-ego. Some authors and researchers claim that one's self-talk is often similar to the way one's parents spoke to them as children – they mirror each other. The development of the super-ego is very important since internalizing good boundaries and prudent judgment is a necessary feature of being an adult. Things like "don't cross the street before looking", and "be friendly and polite, don't be rude!" are important super-ego restrictions to the wild and capricious desires and forces of the child-like id. The problem is that if there was abuse, or negative parental input, or traumatic life events, kids can internalize an unhealthy set of self-critical beliefs and attitudes that get expressed by an unbalanced 'monster' of a super-ego.

Some people actually hear their inner negative critical voice as a voice from a real person they had contact with in the past. For many, this can be a dead relative, or caregiver, or a childhood influence. The voice of their inner critic became internalized and it continued to dominate them into adult life.

Not all people with an excessively self-critical inner voice acquired that voice in early childhood. For some, they acquired it via an intense experience, or through friendships, or from a particularly stern boss at work that once fired them, or even because of other factors and habits. Some people acquire their inner critical voice like an heirloom from those they loved and admired most, and if they do not recognize that their acquired self-critical habits are actually toxic they may go on associating that inner voice with automatic feelings of comfort and idealization that thinking of that beloved person generates within them.

The fact is that the onset and cause of NST can come from many different factors, not just childhood personalities and parents. The onset can happen for a variety of reasons, but the progression and development of the habitual tendency to engage and believe in one's negative thoughts about ourselves and the world around us are gradual and cumulative. From previous chapters, particularly chapter 1 and chapter 2, we learned that NST is likely to lead to more NST in a negative cycle of feedback.

So, aside from childhood, what are the other ways that people might begin to develop an unhealthy inner critical demon? That is what I will explore in the very next section.

COMMON UNSKILLFUL HABITS THAT CAN LEAD TO NST

Many different habits can actually lead to the onset and development of an unhealthy and dominant inner critical voice.

Leaving Relationship Problems Unresolved

Our relationships, particularly our romantic relationships, are often the most impactful and personal factors in our psychological and physical health. Our relationships tend to be mirror-like in that they feedback our inner worlds back to us through our partner and vice versa. All relationships have their strong and weak areas, and it stands to reason that if couples don't work on their weak areas or resolve their problems together constructively then unsurprisingly relationships can become rather toxic for both parties. Indeed, if relationship problems are avoided and remain unresolved then they can lead to many other problems, one of which can be pathologically negative self-talk.

Many people avoid conflict in relationships even to the extent that they avoid raising their personal needs and issues. The habit of avoiding unresolved discontent and problems in a relationship can actually intensify negative feedback loops and feelings of resentment, anger, depression, worthlessness, and many other issues. In certain emotionally abusive relationships that are characterized by narcissism and co-dependency (a vast and complex topic in and of itself that is way beyond the scope of this work) people can often develop an extremely toxic inner dialogue where they often become cognitively dissonant, guilt-ridden, and inappropriately assume the blame for all the failures in the relationship which leads to debilitating depression and destruction erosions of self-worth.

Even if people are not in the midst of a pathologically abusive relationship (physical or emotional) the habit of avoiding relationship problems and leaving them unresolved can escalate into traumatic experiences and maladaptive mechanisms of coping which can cause habits like NST to arise. This is because NST is basically an addictive pattern of negative thinking and feeling.

Relationships have the potential to provide immense fulfillment, social support, and opportunity for expressions of love and self-worth, but more often than not people's unresolved psychological issues combine to make relationships a breeding ground for negativity and denial, negative self-talk, and suffering.

Facing relationship problems directly and working with your partner is one of the most empowering things you could do to prevent yourself from developing NST or making it worse. The potential positive benefits of a healthy, balanced mature relationship are worth making the effort.

Poor health habits

If you don't feel good physically, you eat poorly, you live in high-stress situations, sleep poorly, and suffer from chronic fatigue, brain fog, or some other chronic condition then it can be extremely difficult to have inner clarity and a healthy inner critic. The bottom line is that looking after your physical and mental health is essential to living a happy fulfilled life. Taking care of your health will make it far less likely to develop bad NST habits as well as make it much easier to tackle an already present inner critic and transform it into something positive and beneficial. Neglecting your personal health will definitely lead to a multiplication of problems in your life which would give fuel to your inner critic and make it stronger.

Finding a healthy lifestyle that works for you is a critical way to prevent NST and reverse your negative habits. In fact, part of living healthily is to no longer engage in negative self-talk. But, having a healthy body acts as an important positive factor as a basis for everything else you do. Healthy lifestyles usually involve proper sleep, reducing stress, getting good nutrition, and exercising 3-5 times a week. Apart from generating calm clear emotional states, living healthily protects you from horrible diseases and conditions and acts as a solid foundation for a fulfilling life.

Excessive Social isolation

This factor has been particularly relevant in a COVID world and it will likely remain a major factor in the 'new normal' of the post COVID19 world too. Social isolation is actually very beneficial for people because it allows people to reduce their stressors and come into contact with themselves directly without distraction – solitude can be deeply calming and grounding. Unfortunately, if solitude is used in an unhealthy way to avoid the stress one has due to commitments or social anxiety, then it can be a little addictive and avoidant.

When people spend unhealthy or excessive amounts of time alone it can actually make your NST worse. This is because without others to compare your inner dialogue to you can fall into a cycle of rumination and downward spiraling negativity. Other people help give us a point of comparison by which we can be a little more objective about our inner dialogue. This comparison helps us to notice when our self tlk is toxic and negative and prevents us from always automatically believing it to be true. The other benefit of being with people as opposed to excessively spending time alone is that we have the opportunity to distract from our negative self-talk which can be a welcome relief and create a little distance and space within us from the negative inner critic.

Spending time with well adjusted healthy friends can be very healing, and affirming. We can always reach out to our friends for emotional support should we need it and we can get a sense of our own self-worth and beauty as a person through our interactions with the people that actually appreciate us and our efforts.

Being on your own makes all your dialogue internal. If your internal dialogue is already negative, then too much time alone will definitely lead to an intensification of negative criticism that can spiral into poor mental and physical health outcomes. Don't underestimate the value of a few good friendships – social contact extends the life span, reduces stress, and gives us an arena to practice being positive internally and externally. Just being around others can actually reduce negative thoughts.

Never asking for help – even when you really need it

Many people with a habit of engaging in NST find it difficult to reach out to others and ask for help and support. This is often because they don't believe they deserve loving compassionate treatment, or they want to live up to their inner critic's ideals of perfection where asking for help is seen as 'weak' and 'flawed'.

Asking for help when you need it is healthy and maturely acknowledges your own limitations. It also creates opportunities for social contact which can be immensely beneficial. If you don't ask then you are very likely to never receive any help – how would people know? This lack of spontaneous offers for help can actually sometimes feed into negative patterns of thoughts that aim to prove how undeserving and worthless you might feel you are. If no one offers to help you, then you might be unconsciously using that fact as a kind of proof that no one cares for you. The truth is that asking for support when you need it is a mature and healthy response to facing personal difficulties.

It is important to realize that asking for help is appropriate and healthy in the right situations. If you never ask for help it can definitely contribute to negative states and NST – making it worse. Most people who live under the oppressive tyranny of their inner critical voice find it very difficult to ask for help, so just changing this one behavior and making the effort to reach out can have massive benefits.

Neglecting You and Not making Space for "Self-Care"

This goes beyond looking after your physical health. Self-care in this context means taking the time to prioritize your own wishes and desires above the needs of those around you. This is an important part of balancing your needs with those of others, particularly dependents like your children or spouse. If people don't make enough 'me time' for themselves then they leave themselves vulnerable to negative patterns of self-talk. Making an effort to explicitly give yourself 'me time' gives your body and mind a clear message that you feel like you are worthy of your own attention and that your needs are valuable and important to you.

A lot of NST revolves around feeling like a selfish person or completely uncaring of others' needs. Many parents find it quite hard to balance their own needs against the needs of their children often feeling guilty if they take any time out for themselves. This is a poor pattern of negative self-talk and doesn't acknowledge your own value and worth to yourself – which can just fuel resentment and frustration along with poor self-worth.

It is necessary, appropriate, normal, and healthy to take some time for yourself and your own goals in between being a superstar for everyone else.

Denial of Your own Negative Self-talk

It is normal to hear your inner critic from time to time. Balanced self-criticism is important for being able to learn from mistakes and grow and develop as a person from strength to strength. Balanced self- criticism can help you to become aware of your maladaptive defensive behavior and prevent those kinds of behaviors from getting in your own way. Your inner critic, when balanced and appropriate, helps you to navigate within your own boundaries and negotiate your social connections and real-life commitments with clarity and efficacy – it can help you.

But, ignoring or denying your own psychological peccadillos can lead to a form of negative feedback which can make negative self-talk worse. For example, if you are in the habit of being overly defensive when people challenge your behavior of beliefs, and you insist that you don't have any negative self-talk then they may get worse.

If you do not authentically acknowledge the kind of dialogue that typically runs through your head as negative when it is negative then you will prevent yourself from eliminating it you're your mind altogether. This means that you will be vulnerable to all the negative consequences of NST that we explored in Chapter 2. The stakes are pretty high, so denying the truth about yourself holds you in negative states indefinitely and you might realize that upon reflection the price of temporary relief that you get by denying your negative habitual tendencies is not worth paying considering the massive benefits of facing and successfully resolving those tendencies.

Keeping Bad Company

If you find yourself constantly spending your time with negative people then it is likely you will go on to develop negative habitual patterns of thinking. Just being around negative people can have a draining effect on our energy and moods. If your current friendship group is characterized by toxic negativity then chances are your thoughts and relationships are contributing to negativity within you. If your friends and acquaintances constantly put you down then it is definitely time to seriously reevaluate those friendships and drop the ones that don't serve you and move on to different vistas. This is actually a part of healthy living and self-care. The hard decision to leave toxicity behind you might feel heartbreaking. You might even have negative thoughts about doing that, thoughts that paint you as a horrible person, who abandons their friends and doesn't care about others. But, the reality is that if you really value yourself and want to change your internal dialogue and external circumstances you should consider changing the dynamic of your friendships to transform them into healthy ones, or, failing that, leave them and move on.

Just as being in a toxic relationship can be extremely damaging to body and mind, so it is with toxic friendships. Staying in dysfunctional friendships will definitely increase your negative patterns of thought and behavior, particularly over time.

Surrounding yourself with positive people is actually quite a good strategy for personal success and fulfillment and happiness. The people with whom you keep company form a major part of your world and contribute significantly to your inner dialogue about your success, self-worth, and happiness.

LAST THOUGHTS ON THE CAUSES OF NST

If you take an honest look at your life and authentically acknowledge the sources and causes of your personal negative habits, then you will be in a great position to do something about them. Whether you internalized a critical voice from your childhood or suffered the consequences of a traumatic relationship later in adult life the truth is it is never too late to start making constructive changes in your life to boost your positivity and grow your sense of self-worth. It is important to be kind to yourself, engage in healthy living, make time or self-care, reach out to positive friends, and engage in positive influences. Ask for help if you need it, or seek it out from professional sources – there is no shame whatsoever in doing whatever you need to do to break your own negative patterns of behavior. Ultimately it is so utterly rewarding and beneficial to systematically drop those influences in your life that do not serve your highest potential – be smart, kind, loving, and compassionate to yourself for a change. Summon your courage to finally do the right thing and drop all those factors that undermine your happiness and efforts to lead a fulfilled life.

Identifying the negative factors that cause and contribute to pathological negativity in your life is a huge step towards actually changing your inner dialogue to one of positivity and success.

5

DETHRONING THE TYRANT

HOW TO CHALLENGE YOUR NEGATIVE SELF-TALK

Ultimately we will be looking at ways to transform your negative inner critical voice into a voice that supports you – a best friend with great analytical skills. But, before you can change or transform this 'inner negative tyrant' you do need to be aware of it inside you first. If you are aware and vigilant and can notice the inner critic as it surfaces and talks within you, then you will be able to challenge and eliminate the habit of validating the stream of negative thinking and criticism that comes from this nasty tyrant.

This chapter explores methods to dethrone that tyrant – how to challenge it and stop your habitual negative patterns of thinking. Later chapters will deal with skillful methods to transform the tyrant into something beneficial, a companion worthy of your skills and goals.

So, before we begin, it is worth noting that to challenge your critic it is necessary to first be aware of it – something we have explored in earlier chapters. If you are in the habit of ignoring your inner critic or denying that you have negative thoughts that bring you down then this habit of denial and ignorance must be broken first. The first step is to acknowledge your inner critical voice, notice that it is operating in a wild and untamed way, look for patterns in the way it seems to express itself, identify your tyrant's style of negativity, and then start to challenge its dominance by creating distance inside yourself from that voice – finally challenging it based on several skillful methods like reality testing, dis-identification, and other skillful means.

The Process:

Awareness | Detachment & Dis-identification | Challenge

There is a useful stepwise process that most efficiently leads to successfully challenging your inner negative critic. As mentioned above it starts with awareness of when your critic is operating on you and then recognizing the kind of voice and style it has. To be able to do these two things skillfully it can be helpful to go and review the material covered in chapter 1 and chapter 3 again. Chapter 1 describes different types of NST which will give you a working vocabulary of labels to work with, and chapter 3 will help you to pin down when your inner voice is actually operating, name it and pin it down. This constitutes the first phase of successfully challenging the tyrant within.

The process of challenging the inner tyrant actually starts with detaching and dis-identifying from it as a healthy part of you. Most people hear the extremely negative words of their inner voice and identify with it as if they were the one speaking. The inner critic may be using words like "I", or "they", or "me". If your critic is using words like these it implies that you identify yourself as the critic itself. The danger of identifying with the critic as yourself is that you will tend to believe whatever it says without question since it comes from you. To break the hold of the inner critical voice you will need to realize that they are mostly just automatic triggered thoughts that arise in a negative pattern.

Practicing watchfulness or mindful witnessing meditation can help to create a little space and distance within from the voice within you. Meditation that trains silent observation of internal states helps to see the inner critic's monologue for what it is – a simple stream of words with no power, coming from nowhere and going nowhere. Meditating will allow you to catch it as it arises, and then watch it as it happens without comment or injury.

Make it a Separate Entity: Naming it and Speaking in the Second or Third Person

Awareness and presence begin the process of seeing the truth that your inner critic is separate from who you really are. Some psychologists actually recommend that you give your inner critical voice a name, like "Nancy" (negative Nancy), or some other name unrelated to your name or anyone important to you that you know. Naming your inner critic explicitly creates distance between you and it, lessening its power and preventing yourself from automatically believing what it says and internalizing its toxic negativity.[1] Naming your inner hypercritical voice can help you to stop seeing yourself as the problem. Naming it to help you make the distinction - this can stop us from looking at ourselves as the problem.

Another method that can help to create a little separation and dis-identification with your inner negative voice is to respond to it or talk about it in the second or third person. If you refer to it in the third person you will use language like "It, she. He, they, or [Nancy] (insert the name you have given to it)". An example could be, "Nancy is my inner over-critical voice, it/he/she/they always think it/he/she/they know best but really, Nancy is very negative". The second person is using language between you and another person. Typically you refer to things using words like "you", "we", or "us". An example could be, "Hey, don't you think we would both be much happier if you kept quiet for the next few hours? Thank you, let's work together to have a great day rather than obsess with every single insignificant little negative detail, OK with you?". Speaking directly to your inner voice in the second person or speaking about your inner voice in the third person can help with creating inner distance and separation from it. Whenever 'Nancy' starts acting up, just tell her to sit in a corner and whisper to the wall, you're busy getting your awesome on![2]

Reality Testing – Thoughts and Words are Not Reality Itself

Thoughts and feelings are expressions of belief and attitude about reality, they can be true or false. The reality itself filled with you, your body, the immediate environment, and sensory streams in consciousness, these things are solid, real, imminent, and usually much more reliable as sources of information (provided you don't suffer from any problematic hallucinations or delusions). What can be true or false about the sky, the sun, or a bird singing? On the other hand, critical word statements and imagery are simply fantasy (imagery) or prone to be either true or false. If something could be false then it is important to check in with reason and think about the statements the critic is spewing out – most of the time the statements won't hold up to any questioning because they aren't rational at all, they tend to be based in irritation subconscious automatic conditioning and beliefs given to you by your experiences or what other people told you during your formative years. If you check in to reality and ask questions like, "Is that really true?", or, "how do you know that?", or even better, "Who are you?", or "I would never say that about myself, you must be an imposter!".

Just remember that thoughts and feelings fluctuate all the time, they aren't the kind of things that cannot be challenged and they should be automatically accepted as potent sources of true and factual information about who and what you are as a person. You can challenge the thoughts that strike you as negative by asking how true each negative statement is – put each of these thoughts under the scalpel, cross-examine them. Then see negative thoughts from an outside perspective – would you agree with a friend who was saying that about themselves?[3]

Challenge: Set Some Limits

You are the boss in your inner mental world, not the critical tyrant. Some counseling experts have suggested explicitly setting limits on the time your negative critical tyrant gets to be active within you. Outside of the allowed time, simply crush your thoughts and move to other ones, don't even listen. But during that time frame, e.g. an allowed 30 minutes or an hour after lunch, just practice watching and observing that voice run its course without changing or identifying with it – note how powerless that voice is without your reactions to it.

Note too that the thoughts and words of the inner critic arise, sustain themselves for a bit, and then fade away to nothing all by themselves. They only stay if you feed them reactivity and acceptance or belief.

Responding to your inner voice, acknowledging it, is completely different from arguing with it. Arguing with it or believing it without question amounts to the same thing. It amounts to feeding it with energy making it stronger and more toxic.

On the other hand, watching it, allowing it to operate on your terms, and responding to it if necessary by correcting where it is factually lying to you and trying to get you to believe it, is mature and constructive. Acknowledging and responding is a great way to bring the negative thought patterns from the habitual automatic subconscious realm up into the conscious aware and empowered realm of your bright and aware mind. Fighting with that voice and arguing is just entering its world, not asserting yours.[4]

Setting limits ends up limiting the damage that this negative inner voice can actually cause. It also asserts your own inner sovereignty over your mind and self-concept, and finally, limits can make the voice powerless because you are ready and waiting to watch it try to do its thing even though it is powerless – sometimes the attempts of this negative critic to get you to feel bad become almost laughable, humorous, ridiculous – they may make you laugh because of how silly the voice is actually being. Give your voice an hour a day, or limit it to a certain space or room or section of your life – this will completely defang the monster and reveal how powerless it actually is.

Challenge: Reduce Urgency and Importance

Your inner tyrannical critical voice will always try to convince you that what they're saying is important, true, and urgent. You can combat the tendency of this critical voice to sound important, urgent, and true whenever it exaggerates your negatives or the negatives in any situation.

Simply ask yourself whether the issue this inner critic thinks is so important will really be that important in five years. I mean is this apparently negative thing really that negative in the larger scheme of things? Is it worth worrying over considering I probably don't really care that much and will just forget about it in the next hour, let alone in five years?

Another way to defuse the inner critical voice is to constantly remind yourself that you are a small part of a huge world – Honestly speaking, how important really is this issue that the inner critical voice is nattering on about now? Is it really worth the bother and negativity giving time and energy to this apparently 'serious' negative problem with me or my situation? In the great scheme of things you realize that many of your worries just don't make any sense – the energy and happiness you lose by focusing on insignificant pseudo-problems are just not worth it.

Say It Out Loud & Thought Stopping

One strategy you can use is to devise a way to stop your negative thoughts in their tracks – making clear inner mental space for other things to happen in your world. A great method to do this is to repeat what the inner negative voice is nattering about out loud to yourself and then reflect on it. This often stops that voice in its tracks because it brings the internal toxic narrative fully into the conscious mind where it cannot hide from its own folly.

Another good way to stop the run of negative trains of thought is to make some kind of signal that you can show yourself to jolt your awareness to help you stop indulging in your negativity. You could make a little stop sign and flash it at yourself, or ring a tiny little bell, or whistle, o anything unusual that makes a sound or has a striking visual image or action associated with it. This is very effective because it jolts your mental activity and brings attention to something else. Eventually, you associate the thing that you use with stopping negative thoughts, such that they instantly stop. This method can be quite fun and I encourage you to get creative in finding something that works for you.

Watch For Patterns –Keep a Journal Down

Watch your inner critical tyrant closely, look especially for when it arises, and what it does when it happens. A great way to discover patterns in this inner critical voice is to keep a daily journal where you write down your experiences and observations of the tyrant. After a month you can go over your recorded observations and look for patterns in the voice, see if common things trigger it, or if it says similar things repetitively. This process can be very interesting and revealing. The act of writing about your inner voice in the third person can also help keep it distant from you and your sense of self – creating healthy detachment and dis-identifying from it as 'you' and your problem. Things that you might notice could be that it comes out in the company of others, or that it always tries to punish you whenever you want something really nice for yourself, or when your partner is around. Sometimes you might discover that it only comes out to try to be negative about you or the world when you are overtired. This information can be very critical to you since if you know it happens when you are tired you can prioritize getting regular good sleep and prevent your negative inner critic from having any power over you.[5] Remember, the negative inner voice is almost always exaggerating or false, finding its pattern can completely destroy the illusion it weaves inside your head and free you from thinking it has anything useful to say when it's being negative.

Being able to challenge and dethrone your inner tyrant is an amazing skillful 'step-up' from being a victim to its negativity. If you can manage to be aware, recognize it, name it and describe it, find the pattern, observe it's ridiculous attempts to pull you into its web, then you can challenge it directly on the lies it tries to make you believe about the world and yourself. You can even crush it into silence by stopping the train wreck of cascading negative thoughts if you get creative and make yourself a signal and practice. Challenging the voice that spews forth toxicity with you feels really empowering and you should see drastic positive changes in your life unfold automatically as you get better and better at doing it. Start off gradually and slowly, progress is key. In time, one small challenge leads to another, until your efforts snowball your results and you begin to reclaim the space in your mind as your own kingdom to rule. Your kingdom can be positive and beneficial, and it begins with challenging that damned negative voice within.

6

FROM TYRANT TO FRIEND

TRANSFORMING THE INNER VOICE

Having come this far it's time to look at how to go one step further than stopping or challenging your negative inner voice. Eliminating negativity is an amazing achievement, but why stop there? Remember back to chapter 2 where I described that one of the consequences of NST was that you miss out on all the benefits of positive self-talk (PST)? That is what we will really aim for in this book, first to eliminate your negative habits of self-talk, but then to go one step further and transform that negative inner voice into a friend. That inner voice which was always so critical and self-defeating actually has a few qualities which we should not lose. A critical voice can be a very good advisor and a friend provided it works for our benefit and comes with a positive outlook. Being critical requires wisdom and intelligence - these things shouldn't be thrown out, but rather cultivated and nurtured into something positive. Adding a positive inner dialogue to your mind will help you to reap the benefits of positive self-talk. Having a wise and discerning inner voice that works on your behalf will be of immense benefit.

As a necessary condition to rewiring or reprogramming yourself to have a positive inner voice, you will need to have significantly eliminated and challenged your negativity. From that point of departure, we can continue in this chapter by looking at ways to change your negative self-talk into something more positive. I will explore different skillful methods like cognitive restructuring, different ways you can change your internal dialogue, visualization and meditation techniques, and leveraging a healthy lifestyle.

STEPS TO GRADUALLY REWIRING YOUR BRAIN – EDUCATING THE INNER VOICE

The overall idea in this chapter is to gradually shift that inner negative voice towards becoming positive. We don't want to attempt to 'flip a switch' and have a negative voice all of a sudden become completely positive – that doesn't work.

What is effective is slowly edging and nudging that inner voice towards being something positive and friendly, astute, and decisive. Hold its hand and nudge the inner critic as you would slowly educate a child. A gradual approach is important here for a few reasons. The first good reason to take a gradual approach is that in many cases the little changes you start seeing over time give you great feedback and positive motivation to keep going – each small success feels great and makes the next small success more likely. Another great reason is that trying to aim for final and complete success right of the bat is similar to emphasizing perfectionism – all or nothing. We want to eliminate that kind of pressure and work gently, gradually, and with maximum compassion. We aren't at war with our inner critic, it is a legacy of our past history, instead, we want to rewire the habitual negative tendency of negative thinking and transform it – building new neural connections, new ways of thinking, and new habits. Habits take time to entrench and learn, rewiring the brain takes consistent effort daily - this means that we should take a gradual approach. The final reason why taking a gradual approach is preferred to a sudden approach is that it simply works. For the rest of the chapter, I want to introduce skillful methods that will help to gradually nudge your inner critic towards becoming positive and beneficial. These methods will really help rewire your brain by reinforcing habits that serve you and unwire habits that don't. Each has its place and each method is best done daily without break for as long as it takes to feel significant benefits.

A gradual approach that is going to be successful at rewiring your neural-networks (the way you habitual tendencies are wired in your brain) requires consistency (a little every day) much more than it does erratic efforts of great intensity (a lot of effort in one go followed by doing nothing for several days followed by huge effort again).

From Creating Distance to Changing its Tone

In the last chapter, you learned how to challenge your negative tyrant and its pathological thinking patterns directly. One of the best methods to do that was to create distance within yourself and stop identifying with that negative voice as your own. Speaking about that voice in the 2nd or 3rd person, writing about your critic in a journal, practicing watchful meditation, and naming the voice were all great ways of creating this space, however, now it's time to try something a little different, changing the tone of the voice.

What do I mean by this? I mean that in addition to having the distance you are working to create, now try to also change the tone of that voice from something harsh and judgmental to something gentler, kinder. You can do this by pointing out to the voice in your head that it is being harsh, mean, rude, or judgmental. Then you can suggest back to that voice how you would prefer it expressed itself to you. Instead of saying "you're such a failure, look how you always bungle things!", you can say to it, "I did very well and I can learn from where I didn't handle the situation as skillfully as I maybe could have. Please tell me where I could improve, and what I did well so that I can do better next time because I will do better next time".

Speaking out loud was a great method that I shared with you in the last chapter which helps to interrupt negative thinking and create distance from the tyrant within. In the context of shifting the tone of the inner critic, speaking aloud can also be very useful – many people find that doing that helps make their attempts at shifting the tone of the inner critic more successful.[1]

Shifting from Analysis to Observation and Validation

Our inner critic is judgmental; it critiques the 'parts' and exaggerates those 'parts' negatively. This means that it is like a pathological mental analyzer – it takes small parts of the whole, makes them important, shows them in deficient negative light, and judges you for having those parts.

Particularly toxic inner critics will also mock your efforts to improve the parts that they highlight to you, and the most toxic ones will mock your successes because those parts weren't problematic in the first place.

Basically, there is no 'winning' against a toxic inner critic IF you play the game of analysis that it plays. If you play the same game your inner negative critic is playing, you will never be able to end the game and change its voice to something positive and beneficial. That is why arguing with your inner critic is never a good idea. I mentioned that a better approach you could take is to be responsive to your inner critic, but not to argue with it. Another suggestion I made was to observe it mindfully and watch it without judgment. Why would watching your critic with full attention have a beneficial effect? What watching or witnessing does do for you is that it basically witnesses the inner critic but fails to play the game it wants to play with you – it does not feed the inner critic what it needs to continue on doing what it's doing.

What is great about witnessing your critic? Watching your critic, if done with a detached observational awareness that does not have any judgment, nor desire to change the critic, tends to transform the nature of the critic and remove the urgent powerful hold it may have. The same is true about watching one's emotions. Our emotional responses to the inner critic's chain of negativity are what ultimately fuels the inner critic to become stronger.

Disturbing negative emotional states cause us to become stressed, anxious, cognitively unclear, defensive, afraid, and more likely to believe the inner critic and be unable to discern the truth – it impairs your ability to reality test. Mindful observation of emotions helps to simply see them as they arise, then acknowledge that they are there, you'll see them stay awhile then they transform or fade and dissolve by themselves.

If you train yourself to watch and observe your emotional states as they arise then they will no longer have such a compelling hold over you. How does one achieve the ability to just watch emotions without being 'taken over' by them? [2]

The answer is to simply practice looking inwardly by adopting a mindfulness meditation practice.

How to 'Do' Mindfulness

Mindfulness practice is something you do to get better at training your powers of observation, particularly of being AWARE of your internal states. Your internal states are all the sensations of body, imagery and word thoughts in the head, and emotions (often felt as sensations in positions in the body). The thing that makes mindfulness practice so powerful is that you train to be aware of all the above internal states whilst also being aware of the external world and performing the activities in your daily life. It turns out that being aware of the total inner world and still being able to go about your day without being distracted and losing focus is quite difficult. Fortunately, you don't have to master the ability to do this straight away, you only really need to practice sitting quietly with yourself and gradually adding layers to what you pay attention to.

The simplest approach is often the most effective approach, so I recommend the basic simple practice of sitting being aware of your breath for 20-30 minutes five days a week. This is something to build up to.

- First, **choose a quiet place and time** where you won't be disturbed by too much noise or external activities, and no one will come calling for you. **Sit with a relaxed comfortable posture**, either in a chair or comfortably cross-legged on the floor.
- Next, **bring your awareness to your breathing**. Don't change the way you breathe or interfere with it in any way, **just notice it**. If you find you are compelled to control your breathing and don't know how to let your body just 'do its thing' then It sometimes helps to imagine that air falls into the lungs and then tumbles out instead of you making effort to pull in and push out.
- Stay with your breath and remain still in mind and body. If you find your attention gets distracted by

thoughts in your head or by thinking of the future or past or anything other than simply watching the breath, then bring yourself gently back to the breath. It can help in the beginning to count your in and out breaths – in 1, out 2, in 3….out 10. When you get to 10 start the next in-breath at 1 again. If your mind wanders, don't worry, just bring your attention gently back to the breath and start at 1 again. Don't judge yourself for losing focus, it's actually quite normal for people to wander off into other places in their head, everyone finds it a little difficult until they get used to it. Just bring your attention back to your breath and resume the count from 1.

- In the beginning, start with 5-minute sessions, then increase that time to 10minutes, then 15minutes, until finally, you can handle 20 minutes of gentle calm-abiding while watching the breath. This might sound really easy, but don't be fooled by the simplicity of the practice, 5 minutes of calm focused attention on the breath can often feel like an eternity, especially if you have a busy mind. Most people with highly active negative critical voices in their heads have busy minds, so it is quite common to have difficulty in the beginning. The point is to not worry about your progress but to relax and enjoy the process. In no time you will find that it is such a pleasant thing to do that even 30minutes doesn't satisfy you!

The above practice might sound really simple but that doesn't mean it isn't powerful or that it won't have profound effects on your brain. Mindfulness practices only really show concrete effects if you do them for a minimum of 20minutes five days a week. This means that to find out if this really works for you, you will have to stick with it moving from five minutes initially to 20minutes by the end of one month.

Try increasing the time you sit with your breath by five minutes every week. That way, by the beginning of the fourth week you will be up to 20 minutes; and by the end of that week, you will feel the benefits very strongly indeed. The benefits include stress reduction, clearer focus, mental clarity, diminished emotional disturbance, increased cardiovascular health, and better length and quality of sleep.

Now, how does all this apply to the process of moving from analyzing emotions to validating them? The main link between watching your breath and validating your emotions is awareness in observation practice. The process of focusing attention on emotions in real-time gets easier as you practice with your breath, particularly over time as you practice. When your emotions come flaring up during the day, or in response to your inner critic you will be perfectly placed to try just watching what happens without interfering – just like how you would watch your breath informal mindfulness practice. Then instead of analyzing how you feel, why you feel, or whether you need to feel differently, you just let them be within you and observe them arise, stay, and fall away of their own accord. If you can do that it sends two great messages to your brain. The first message it sends to your brain is that it is OK to feel what you feel in every moment you don't need to feel distressed or agitated by the emotions that arise. The second message that doing this will send to your brain is that the priority response in any moment to emotions is to allow them to arise and retain awareness – instead of engaging with defensive anxious fight-or-flight anxiety responses. The more often your brain gets these messages the more your brain rewires how it handles disturbing emotions, and the more you become master of your reactions to emotional states, the less power your inner critic has to convince you that you are worthless, or that you should get angry with someone, or that you should do something because of the way you feel.

Acknowledging yourself instead of reacting and attempting to change yourself of the world around you is a potent way of saying, "I accept who I am, I am enough". The power of the inner critic's negativity starts to dissolve because you no longer fuel it with negative emotional states that lead to reactive anxiety.

Shifting From "Habitual" to "Intentional"

One great way to shift your automatic unconscious negative self-talk into something more conscious and way more beneficial is to combine setting limits on when you allow your inner critic to talk along with making sure your inner critic engages in self-reflection rather than critical self-judgment. Setting a specific time each day or week to sit down and reflect on your behavior, events, and feelings to constructively identify aspects of improvement and little successes will really bring good benefits over time. Shifting to an intentional way of being can really shift the negative critic into a positive voice the recognizes little gains and constructive identifies areas of challenge that can bring growth. This makes the critic serve you instead of you serving the critic.

Substitution as Replacement

Exchanging your negative inner thoughts and judgments directly for positive statements and encouragement is a great technique to gradually shift your inner negative voice to serve you. Now, instead of negative thoughts being cues for more negativity, they become cues for positivity because you use them as a signal to say positive things to yourself whenever you catch them happening. Critical thoughts can be replaced with encouragement. Instead of saying, "I'm terrible at math" you could say, "I can work at math a little every day until I can say I'm better at math today than I was yesterday".

Modify the intensity

You can alter very intense negative statements like "I HATE XYZ..." to something less negative like, "I don't really like...", likewise you can intensify 'luke-warm' statements about your successes. For example "I did alright..." can be more encouraging and intense when you say, "I really did well compared to how I thought I was going to do".[3]

Reach out To Psychotherapy or Adopt Psychotherapeutic Methods

Some people feel completely overwhelmed by their own negative emotional states and internal dialogue that they feel they cannot gin control over their negative self-talk without professional help. In extreme cases like this, it is completely appropriate to reach out to a professional and engage with psychotherapy to help yourself out of your negativity – that is highly recommended.

However, not everyone may feel like they need such measures, or they might not be in a position to get psychotherapy. In this case, you can try adopting some simple techniques from CBT (cognitive behavioral therapy) to help yourself.

Cognitive Restructuring – (the ABCDE model)

Cognitive Restructuring (CR) is a clinical tool designed for people who are undergoing CBT. It is essentially a step by step way to overcome negative beliefs and patterns of thinking. CR comes in five basic stages from A to E. These stages are called A – Activating Event; B – Belief; C-Consequence; D-Dispute; E-Effect. Every time you feel negativity coming on and it happens in response to some event, then going through these five phases carefully will really help unbind your emotional conditioning. The process aims to restructure your sponsoring beliefs so that you no longer become triggered by simple situations and events.

A - Activating Event:

This is an event that triggers some strong negative emotional responses. Identifying one's triggers or activating events is usually the first step in overcoming those triggering events.

B – Belief:

An activating event, or trigger, cannot be triggering negative emotional responses unless it is accompanied by a pre-existing belief – in this context, the belief is negative and irrational. Based on such a sponsoring belief the event becomes able to trigger a person into having a negative response. A good example would be if someone offers constructive criticism to you, but you feel rattled and defensive. The trigger is the perceived criticism, and the belief behind it is "I'm worthless, incompetent". People who have no confidence in their worth or abilities often do not handle criticism very well – even if that criticism is constructive and delivered appropriately, kindly, and gently as a way to help you to improve in some areas.

C – Consequence

The consequence is the negative emotional state that arises because of the combination of an activated event and prior irrational belief. Sometimes, in cases of deep post-traumatic stress, or deep trauma, the nervous system can respond in the absence of beliefs (without cognitive involvement). This happens a lot in people with extreme fears (phobias) of specific things that generalize into all things of a certain type. Nevertheless, even if the response is automatic via the nervous system the ABCDE method of CR aims to bring these beliefs to the conscious which helps to make responses less automatic. The consequence in the example above is feeling defensive and rattled and emotionally threatened.

D – Dispute

Dispute is the act of challenging the sponsoring belief by rejecting it with factual statements or exchanging the belief with something positive instead. Here mindfulness practices can really help to be with the belief and lessen the overwhelming nature of the consequence.

E – Effect

Effect is the phase of your restructuring where you make sure to pay attention to any benefits that happen as a result of modifying and questioning your belief in the dispute phase. Measuring your own success is important because it encourages doing it again the next time. Furthermore, feeling good about progress, however small, reinforces a new pattern of behavior. This new pattern is one that challenges negative beliefs and thinking and does not allow it to trigger you.

Working with the ABCDE method is usually done with a mindfulness practice that lets you observe your emotions and beliefs in real-time whilst not attempting to change them. For our purposes, you can extend the mindfulness practice of focusing on the breath earlier to include a portion of the time to focus on feelings and emotions and thoughts too. The main thing to do in that motivation is to count your breath as per usual until you feel your mind and body calm and come to rest. Then surround yourself with an image of a cloak of self-love that holds you and spreads warmth and compassion into your heart and limbs. Then you can sit in that space and allow yourself to feel whatever you are feeling without changing it or attempting to improve it or make it stay or go away. This is particularly helpful as a way to be 'with' emotions during a triggering event because it allows you the mental space to apply the ABCDE method and appreciate the way your efforts prevent extremely aversive responses.[4]

Cognitive Restructuring comes with many reported benefits, the main ones include:[5]

- Clarify and organize your mental processes
- Slow down your responses and thoughts through vigilant practice of the ABCDE method.
- In conjunction with mindfulness, CR helps you to become more aware of your own internal states – even in busy external world circumstances.
- Regain a sense of agency and control in your life because you are no longer the victim of your

unconscious irrational beliefs and fears. Your triggers and negativity no longer control you.
- Improve rational thinking because you get to practice challenging your irrational thoughts in the dispute phase. Identifying your underlying irrational beliefs also helps you to identify irrational thinking in daily life whenever you encounter it.
- Promotes self-reflection rather than over-reaction. Promotes constructive inner dialogue rather than reactive critical thinking.
- CR Breaks negative mental habits that lead to disturbing emotional states and negative self-perceptions.

How to Practice CR

I have mentioned a little bit about disputing the sponsoring thought and identifying triggers. I also mentioned how to go about exploring a simple mindfulness practice to get in touch with your inner states so that you can work with them consciously without being reactive. However, I have not given some tips or advice about how to go about using the ABCDE method when you get triggered in real-time moments. In moments when you do get triggered by your internal critic or some external event then follow the following steps.

1. Pause

Don't speak, or react, or do ANYTHING without putting a good 5-second pause in first. For example, if something happens and you feel defensive or angry then the immediate reaction is often to shout or lash out. Stop that from happening by forcing yourself to pause first. Ask yourself after five seconds, "what is actually happening here, what am I feeling, and how are things progressing from there?"

2. Identify the trigger

Which event that just happened triggered your strong emotional reaction? Now that the strong urge to react cued you to pause and breathe and reflect in real-time, identify the trigger. Ask "who is with me?", "What is happening?", "When did this upset feeling begin within me?", "Where is this happening?". These four questions can help you after the fact too when you decide to constructively reflect on a negative triggering event and try to make sense of it to identify your triggers. Asking who, what, when, and where, can help you to narrow down exactly what the trigger is.

3. Notice your automatic thoughts

Automatic thoughts are usually fast to arise, reactive,

and completely automatic. For example, if someone takes your sandwich from the work fridge you immediately think "why do people always take advantage of me!" or perhaps someone cuts in front of you in the line at the bank and you say "what an absolute JERK!" and you feel angry. These are the kinds of thoughts that are automatic. In CR you want to train yourself to become more and more aware of automatic thoughts that usually go unnoticed. As you get better at catching them you get better at preventing irrational triggers that can start spirals of cascading negativity.

4. Identify and evaluate your emotional reaction

This is a simple two-step process, but it can become tricky because sometimes what we feel is a whole jumble of emotions and it isn't clear what your emotional reaction actually is. If you feel a combination of fear and rage at someone stealing your sandwich because you fear your possessions aren't safe and you feel violated and outraged that someone would mistreat you then note both emotions. The second step after identifying the emotions at play is to rate the intensity of emotion on a scale of 1-10. If your anger is mild give it a '2' if you are apoplectic with rage losing control of yourself and punching things, give your anger a 10/10.

5. Generate alternative thoughts

Once you identify your trigger (stolen sandwich), taken note of your automatic thoughts ("how dare someone do this to me, I'm always being taken advantage of!"), and identified your emotions, "anger mixed with vulnerability and fear, feeling worthless, not respected), then it is time to invent alternative thoughts to your automatic ones. An example, in this case, could be, "someone probably really needed it and knew I wouldn't mind, they haven't gotten around to it yet. Even so, I need to assert my boundaries because I know I am worth asking before taking. That is a minimum standard that works for me because I value my self-esteem and self-worth.

6. Check back into your Emotional Response and rate it again

Notice how you are feeling after coming up with new thoughts to replace your automatic reactive thoughts. Most of the time the intensity of the emotional response will decrease, sometimes some emotions go away altogether. This is important because noticing that your efforts resulted in less reactivity and less emotional stress and intensity can really help you to recognize your success and keep up with the habit of doing CR. New habits are worth it if they bring good results, so step 6 is an important way to prove to yourself that what you are doing is beneficial. Feeling better about your efforts can really help to entrench this new way of being a great supportive habit.

Do a Regular Creative Visualization Meditation[6]

This meditation is distinct from mindfulness meditation because it asks you to actively create imagery in the mind. Some people find this method effective as a way to relax, reduce stress, and come home to their body and mind in a calm manner. A typical visualization is good for deep relaxation and clarity if it is at least 30 minutes long, so make time for 30 minutes in your day to relax and focus.

Follow the guidelines below, or record yourself reading this aloud then play it back to yourself so that you can follow your own words through the guided visualization. If you feel you would like to make your own meditation and imagery feel free to get creative and base your own version on the following one if that would work for you instead.

PART 1: RELAX COMPLETELY

- Find a quiet place where you won't be disturbed so that you can sit or lie down comfortably for half an hour.
- Setting an alarm can be helpful to make sure you get up and resume your day without having to worry during the meditation.
- While seated, or lying down, feel out your body, make sure you are fully relaxed and comfortable. Adjust your posture or stretch any tight muscles. Breathe deeply and find your perfect 'spot'.
- Breathe in and out deeply for a few breaths. Do the breathing slowly to relax your body and mind. When suitably ready and present, bring your awareness to your body. Feel how your body feels from the inside out in the present moment.
- Now, place your awareness and feel the tips of each toe in turn. Feel them from the inside, feel each detail of the skin, nails, the tissues deeper in. Gradually shift your awareness up through your body, feeling each part of your body in the same way, from your ankles to the knees, to the eyelids, and finally ending on the crown of the head. Feel each part from the inside out and the outside in. Do this for the whole body.

- After scanning the whole body for a few minutes ending at the crown of the head, bring your awareness to your breathing. Allow your breath to be as slow as you can, feel the air slide into your lungs and your chest slowly rise, then feel the air glide out and your chest and stomach come back to resting position.
- Every out-breath, imagine each part of your body relaxing even more. Really sink the relaxation into each part of your body. Do this until you feel really calm and relaxed. Once you feel completely relaxed move on to the visualization part of the meditation – everything up to now has been just to bring you into the present moment and relax completely.

PART 2: BEGIN TO VISUALIZE

Using your imagination, imagine sitting alone on a beautiful beach. See yourself sitting on the sand, feel the texture of it between your toes. Hear the sound of the sea wash over you, and smell the fresh sea-salt air. Look out over the water and watch the waves come to shore, the sun sparkling in every wave, the whitewater frothing as the breaker reaches the sand, and the low hiss as the wave slides up the beach until it slows and retreats back into the ocean.

Now stand up and approach the waterline and feel the cold refreshing wetness of the sand, smell the ocean air again, and hear the cry of gulls delightfully playing in the crisp warm sunlight and fishing in the sea. Hear the ocean surge, and another wave crash onto the sand and slide up to flow gently over your feet and between each of your toes and slide around your ankles. The gentle caress of the ocean's kiss as it reaches out and welcomes you to this fresh alive space. Use all your senses, hear things, see things, smell things, reach down and cup the seawater and dip your tongue into it, taste the salty earthiness of the water and fully immerse yourself inside the beachscape.

After some time, you notice another figure calmly walking down the beach in your direction. You are curious, there is no one else around, and you feel drawn to greet them and meet them. You slowly happily walk along the water line towards the approaching figure, maybe it's a person, but perhaps not, the sea spray makes it misty and you can discern a shape, perhaps humanoid, or mythological creature, you can't tell clearly – perhaps you have met before and you get a sense of familiarity, perhaps not. Whatever this person is trust in what comes to you at the moment and 'go with it'. Approaching close take in every detail of their appearance, colors, textures, smells, expressions, size, weight, presence, clothing, posture, absolutely every detail you can in every sense you can. Recognize that before you appearing more clearly now is your inner critical voice, the being itself.

As you approach even closer, watch how you feel inside. They notice you now. How do they respond to you? How do they receive you, how do they judge you? What do they think of you? Now that you are close enough notice that they seem to recognize you, they know about you they have opinions about you. What might they think of you and your life? What might they say to you about where you have ended up, what you have become? Do they think you should be doing something different with your life, or are they happy with what they see and know about you? Do they think you should be doing something different, if so what would they suggest to you?

When ready, urge the being to sit next to you in the sand. Tell them you want to speak. Tell it in your own words that you know it has been doing its best to tell you the truth and help you as best it could. In your own way, ask your critic how it is trying to help. Maybe it always tells you that you are an idiot, hopeless, lazy; maybe it says these things to you because it knows you can do better - it knows you have more potential than you actually realize and work with. Perhaps it only knows how to help you by criticizing you because it learned from others who did that with you when you were a young child? Perhaps it doesn't know any better? Perhaps it has the best intentions but it has a very unskillful way of expressing itself, perhaps it really loves you and cares for your growth and happiness, but it only knows how to mock your weaknesses and belittle you to shake you out of your habitual patterns.

After it tells you how it's been trying to help and what it might want from you, thank it for trying and caring, then tell it that you need it to help you differently - With more kindness and compassion, to share its wisdom constructively and provide encouragement rather than keeping on finding fault with you and sharing negativity. Think of what you would need to hear from it to let the critic become your wisest and best friend, one that counsels you when you need it and gives great advice when you might be missing something or needing it. Maybe you could ask it to praise you for good things that you do when you do them, or suggest ways you could do even better and sparkle and shine.

Speak like this until you know that it understands what you need from it to thrive, and you know what it needs from you to be able to be your best inner friend and support. Now you are set up to help each other grow and thrive in the future. Find a great way to say goodbye, and stand up and leave the being that is your critic there on the shore behind you. Find a great spot on the beach far from the sight of your critic and relax into the sun sand and gulls, re-imagine the sights, sounds, textures, and light. Lie down and close your eyes and just drift calmly happily by the sea on this perfect spring day.

Then, noticing your breathing, bring yourself back gently into the room where you started your visualization. Come back to your body, gently open your eyes and feel the floor under you, solid, stable reassuring. You're back.

Each time you do this visualization you are likely to meet different parts of your critic. Trust that each time will be fresh and constructive, safe, and beneficial. Each time will be different, each time you will get to address something specifically important to you. After doing this visualization enough you can begin to recognize your inner critical voice from different moments in your visualizations and remind it to serve you as you showed it should. Apart from directly working to transform your inner critic, this visualization is really great for total relaxation and creativity too.

Maintain a Positive Healthy Lifestyle

Make sure to skill up on healthy living and make choices that support your body image, your body health, and your mental functioning. Make sure to eat good nutritious food with great nutritional building blocks so that your body has all it needs to build and sustain itself. Regular moderate exercise for 30 minutes, 3-5 times a week has multiple benefits not least of which include reducing stress, improving health, staving off depression, clarifying mental processes, and boosting all-around health.

Socially, surrounding yourself with positive people who also treat themselves with care and compassion are just the kinds of people that can help you to avoid falling into the trap of escalating internal negative speech. Being positive, eating right, exercising, sleeping properly, and spending time with positive people with healthy beneficial interests will set the stage for your success, fulfillment, and happiness going forward. What better way to transform your inner critical voice into a voice of encouragement and benefit to help you navigate the uncertain and exciting journey of your own life?[7]

7

THE CULTIVATION OF KINDNESS

The last chapter explored methods to gradually transform your inner critic into a powerful inner friend. We looked at strategies to systematically nudge that inner voice towards using its skills and insight in a way that expressed encouragement, compassion, and kindness. What else could help that voice to transition into a powerful bet friend filled with kindness and compassion? This chapter looks at exactly that issue. At this point in your journey to positivity what remains is to continue to fuel the transformation of your inner thoughts, emotions, and beliefs into a collection of interconnected beneficial habits of mind. What better way to support the transformation of your inner critical voice into something great than to cultivate an inner environment that is suffused and radiating self-compassion and kindness. To change your NST for good, you will need to have a compassionate relationship with yourself. Such a relationship helps to model and support the transformation of the inner critic permanently. If you manage to develop self-compassion as a habitual way of life, then all you need to focus on is to live in such a way to prevent the return of the negative and hostile inner voice. The subject of chapter 8 is all about preventing the return of the inner tyrant. In this chapter, we explore the foundations of that prevention – self-compassion and self-kindness.

THE KEY TO REAL LONG-TERM CHANGE

Eliminating the habit of negative self-talk will not lead to sustainable long-term change. For that kind of change, you need to develop positive habits to take the place of your old negative ones. In fact, if you manage to develop the right positive habits then those very habits will lead to the generation of yet more positive habits in a feedback loop that wires your brain to become very good at being positive as a basic orientation to life. An analogy might be good here to make this point clear.

Imagine that you have some kind of disease, say cancer, and that you take drastic measures to remove this cancer. Imagine that you are successful at removing all cancer from your body, and everything improves and you're happy about it…for a while.

But, then cancer returns, and you are once again back where you started – except that this time you know that what you tried before will only temporarily cure your condition. If only you could have removed the causes of your cancer, then it wouldn't return ever again.

If the causes of your cancer are your daily habits of behavior, your lifestyle choices combined with you inherited genetics, then perhaps it would be better to remove cancer as a symptom of those causes; then go and remove the causes themselves.

The example above is exactly similar to your patterns of negative self-talk. If the inner critic is your 'cancer' and you remove it, then what is left is your conditioning from childhood (a lot like your psychological genetics). To keep the inner critical voice from returning you will have to inculcate positive habits that prevent your old inherited triggers and psychological mechanisms from gaining hold once again. This is why cultivating an inner environment characterized by self-compassion and kindness is so important – it prevents the expression of your past childhood conditioning that always leads to a rampant and untamed inner critical tyrant.

If you are kind to yourself in all ways that matter, then you create internal conditions that make negative self-talk impossible.

METHODS TO CULTIVATE SELF-COMPASSION

Self-compassion is the art of treating yourself kindly. Research into self-compassionate behavior has repeatedly shown that it is linked to increased psychological well-being. Not only that but cultivating a habit of self-compassion will have positive 'knock-on' effects on your relationships with others too because how you treat yourself definitely reflects how you treat others and how you interpret their motives and actions.[1]

The following simple methods are powerful ways to develop self-compassion gradually:

Treat yourself as you would a small child

While a small child is exploring the world and learning for itself it does best with a healthy amount of clear boundaries coupled with an encouraging, compassionate, informative parenting style. The child needs to feel independent enough to try things out for itself, but it also needs to feel safe enough to realize that nothing serious will happen given that freedom. You would not punish a child for making mistakes or acting without wisdom, rather you would support the child gently, point out relevant facts about the world it would need to know, and be encouraged to try again given what it has learned.

If a child is always punished for the initiative it takes because it ends up making a mess of things, then the child learns that taking its own initiative and relying on its own independence and autonomy is a bad practice – which can lead to paralysis of action and negative beliefs about their own self-worth. A healthy, explorative, and curious nature can be tempered by encouragement and compassion for poor behavior and dangerous results. This is the kind of attitude we can take with ourselves too. Whenever we find ourselves making poor choices that lead to unwanted results, instead of taking a harsh punitive critical stance towards ourselves we can reflect on what we did, identify areas of improvement, update what we know about the world, and do much better in the same situations going forward. But, if you denigrate yourself as a hopeless idiotic failure, then how on earth would you develop any new knowledge, skills, or understanding – eventually you might not even try new things in the first place, which is almost a fate worse than death.

It isn't dying you should be afraid of, but dying after a life not lived – living a life of no regrets takes wisdom and self-compassion.

Practice mindfulness

Time and time again in this book I have introduced and stressed the importance and benefits of developing mindfulness of your inner states. In this context, developing compassion for oneself is greatly enhanced by being present with the inner psychological forces that arise to drive you. Knowing yourself intimately is a great way to inject compassionate responses into your inner dialogue about your apparent failures and shortcomings.

Remember you're not alone

Sometimes the most compassionate thing that you can do for yourself is to acknowledge when you need help. This requires you to acknowledge when you have reached your limits and that you feel overwhelmed and unable to cope. Life is vast and larger than you, so it is inevitable that at some point you will have too many things on your plate and can't manage them all. Other times you might feel completed overwhelmed and crushed by your inner negative voice. In times like these, it is sometimes the most self-caring compassionate thing to reach out to a friend, family member, or professional. Admitting when we need help is not admitting weakness, it shows the strength of character to acknowledge what is currently true about yourself. Reaching out also tells yourself that you are worth helping out, that you believe other people will give you support because, frankly speaking, you are worth supporting. If you don't believe you're worth the support of others, then actually trying to ask for support can completely destroy that false belief. Somewhere, someone out there thinks the world of you. In this book, we are trying to make that someone be you, yourself, but it is always true that someone out there will give you the support and encouragement you need. Even strangers are apt to help people they don't know, it seems to be a basic characteristic of many people that support and collaboration are a way of life worth pursuing.

'Imperfect' is Actually the New 'Perfect'

Allow yourself to be imperfect. In previous chapters, I have talked about perfection and how it leads to out of control chains of negative thinking and critical thought. Imperfection is the reality since perfection is really an abstract idea. Perfection places pressure on yourself to meet criteria that are usually unreasonable. Perfection often puts that same pressure on the people and relationships in your life which can be an extremely negative social factor that injects dysfunction into your social connections.

Being self-compassionate is about accepting yourself, warts and all, where you are. More than that, being self-compassionate is simply, to be honest about who and what and where you are right now, then work constructively with that to benefit yourself and then others.

Look after your physical health[2]

I cannot stress enough how important your daily choices are to your immediate and long term health. If you don't eat properly, or sleep well, if you poison your body, or undermine its beautiful organic systems if you constantly feel stressed, you don't exercise, you are always ill and lacking the basic building blocks to sustain a healthy body and happy mind, then what does that say about how you view your own body and mind. Living a healthy life, adopting a healthy lifestyle, being in shape, being fit, all of those positive factors are really just ways of telling yourself that you love and care about your body and mind.

For example, if you want to lose weight then it can be for many reasons. Perhaps it's for health reasons, or perhaps you want to feel good about the way you look? The truth is, the best reasons for losing weight are the ones that work to sustain you to be motivated to make a loving effort to care for your body and treat it with kindness and care. Being obese is a tough burden for your body to handle, not to mention your mind and social connections too. Choosing to care for your body, living to optimize its function and health, that is something that represents the ultimate in self-compassion. In the end, living a healthy lifestyle is the best way to support clear thinking, great energy reserves, and robust and vibrant positive emotional states. Become aware of what makes you and your body feel great, then do those things.

Spend time doing things you enjoy[3]

This sounds really obvious, why wouldn't people do this. Well, amazingly enough, many people feel guilty about making time to do the things that they really enjoy. People often feel that perhaps they may be being selfish, or that they don't deserve to put their own desires and wishes before other people's needs.

However, what could be more self-loving and kind and self-compassionate than exploring your own interests and developing your own potential, and having fun on your own terms. It is NOT selfish or negative to take time for yourself. Provided you remain responsive to other people's needs in a mature and balanced way, then you absolutely SHOULD be taking time for yourself, preferably every day, or at least a few times a week. If you find that you never have time for yourself consider that you might be operating under a toxic automatic subconscious belief that your needs aren't worth fulfilling. In the end, no one else is responsible for your happiness, this is how it is, and indeed this is the best way it could be because it gives us the freedom to choose our own path of happiness in life instead of those choices being up to others. If you find yourself resenting people around you for being too needy and you find you don't ever do things for yourself, then perhaps you are the reason for that state of affairs. If you find that the choices you make are subtly giving away the chance to fulfill your own dreams consider being compassionate to yourself about that and schedule some time for yourself every week where you get to do whatever you want to do. The essence of self-care is self-compassion. Self-compassion begins with taking responsibility for your own happiness and not allowing yourself to be a victim of your own choices or your own inner critical negativity.

To really be able to spend time doing things you enjoy, you first have to know what you actually enjoy. This means that actively trying to find out what ignites your passion and interest is a worthwhile and compassionate thing to do. Allow yourself to become 'fired up' don't feel shame at your deepest interests and hobbies – the things you are passionate about are the things you can enjoy and share with the rest of us – you'll be doing all the rest of us on this planet a huge favor if you share your passion and pursue it with focus and relaxed enjoyment. That kind of activity really inspires others too, and it will inspire you to feel excited about something in your day when you get up in the morning. When last did you wake up in the morning feeling excited about something that you were going to do in your day?

If it has been a while since you felt anything like 'excitement' in your mornings, then it might be the right time to make an effort to explore new things, expose yourself to new experiences, and discover what 'lights you up'.

Cultivate self-acceptance

"Cultivating self-acceptance" is really just another way of saying "cultivating self-compassion". Self-acceptance and self-compassion are identical bedfellows. Just that one expression emphasizes a different aspect of compassion to the other. Accepting who you are, failings and strengths alike are tantamount to saying, "I think that I am great, as I am". This doesn't mean that you stagnate and no longer seek opportunities to develop your potential and eliminate negative habitual patterns. No, accepting where you are, if done maturely and constructively, leads to an acknowledgment of what you are responsible for, what you can reasonably do right now, and allowing yourself to like and dislike what you genuinely like and dislike. Honestly accepting your current state of affairs is compassionate and empowering, it lets you realistically focus on your dreams by actually acting with the resources at your disposal in the present moment. Self-acceptance is the key to treating yourself like a health explorative child, and it is the key to defusing the negative inner critical tyrant that tries to get to not accept yourself and feel powerless and helpless and worthless. Self-acceptance is literally self-compassion in action. Making sure to practice accepting yourself as you are will be the way that you eventually cultivate an inner environment that is suffused with compassion and positivity which will make the return of your negative self-talk very unlikely.

SPEAK WITH DR. STRONG

If you would like some help from me implementing strategies to help you with your health issues, then I'd like to invite you to speak with me personally.

You can work with me personally or look at my online health coaching course that gives you all the tools you need to thrive rather than merely survive.

Head over to: https://www.stronghealthplan.com/casestudy

There will be a short video and application about your health or what you need help with. (So we can review them before the call).

Answer the questions, and on the next page, you'll see a calendar with a list of available dates and times for your call. Pick the one that works best for you.

Once you have booked your time, the confirmation page will have some instructions on how to prepare for the call. Please review them thoroughly. Watch the video that breaks down what it looks like to work with me. Review the case studies from my clients. That way, when you get on the call, you will already have quite a few of your questions answered.

Once on the call, I will take a look at what you are doing, identify the problems you are having, and see if I can help. If I can help, I will show you what it looks like to work with me. You can then decide if you want to become one of my clients or not.

No pressure, but either way, you will get a lot of clarity out of this call. Visit https://www.stronghealthplan.com/casestudy to book your call today!

8

A BRIGHT FUTURE

PREVENT NEGATIVE SELF-TALK FROM EVER RETURNING

Having come this far you have already discovered many powerful tools and information that will actually enable you to catch, identify, and label your habitual NST. Then beyond catching and identifying your NST you learned skillful techniques to stop it in its tracks and tame the tyrant within. The last skills we explored were skillful techniques to gradually transform your inner voice into a source of positivity – hopefully culminating in you gradually creating a healthy balanced inner friend to provide you with a positive and supportive and insightful narrative for your journey through life.

In this chapter, the final one of this book, we are going to look at how to prevent your inner tyrant from insidiously sneaking back into your life and poisoning your inner dialogues all over again. The truth about your inner critic is that it is a necessary part of you, and if it's working for you instead of undermining you, then that inner voice will be a highly beneficial inner companion to have.

But, like any person in real life, your inner voice will always be prone to falling back into old patterns of behavior. Even though you may have succeeded in transforming your inner voice into something positive, balanced, insightful, and supportive, you will still need to remain compassionate and vigilant and constantly support healthy positive habits of body, speech, and mind to keep your emotions and thoughts functioning well together.

One of the best strategies to prevent negative self-talk from ever returning is to practice self-compassion alongside the techniques linked I presented all throughout this book - techniques that challenge and transform negative patterns of thought and behavior. Self-compassion will therefore be one of the main themes of this brief chapter and we will explore practical methods to cultivate it shortly. Finally, there are also a few important things to be aware of in addition to practicing self-compassion that also significantly prevents the return of negative thinking.

If you digest, integrate, implement, and master the techniques in this final chapter then you are set up for sustaining your own bright future. A future filled with opportunities taken, healthy friendships made, and exciting experiences enjoyed.

It is remarkable how much life can 'open up' to you when you finally stop getting in your own way. You have already felt this to be true about your life having come this far in the book, so now it's time to include the final nuances of an overall plan to promote positive mental habits and prevent you from ever returning to the dark negative self-critical states of mind that you started in.

PRACTICE SELF-COMPASSION

Self-compassion is about putting yourself in a position to acknowledge the positives in your life, become your own best friend, and celebrate every success, even the tiniest ones.

Self-compassion is the wish to orient your attitudes so that you set yourself up for success authentically and realistically. Self-compassion is recognizing that you no longer need to chain yourself to impossible standards of perfection whilst also becoming your own best friend.

There are several practical things that you can do to protect yourself from opening up the door to NST ever again. Practicing self-compassion is related to each one of them, but in the main, being compassionate and friendly with yourself Is an attitude which you adopt to orient yourself constructively towards your own life. It starts with being your own best friend and moves forward by not allowing yourself to be caught by pressurizing unrealistic expectations and standards of perfection.

Being your Own Best Friend

This means talking to yourself with the same care, patience, compassion, and respect as you would your best friend. You would NEVER call one of your best friends a "loser" or "idiot", or a "failure". So why should you do that to yourself? There aren't really any failures, just opportunities for self-reflection, choose to learn, and adopt alternative strategies to succeed. Each obstacle is a process that positively challenges you to develop greater skills of flexibility, analysis, and compassion for your apparent failed attempts on the path to achieving success.

Being your own best friend is also about acknowledging and celebrating your 'little wins' just as your good friends would be really happy for your successes and good fortune. Remembering our successes and celebrating them in our mind's eye really helps to prevent the old inner tyrant from sounding believable when they declare you a 'loser' that won't amount to much. A good friend also makes space for you to be yourself, to fail at things sometimes on the way to succeeding later. A good friend keeps good company – YOU. If you transform your inner voices into the best of your friends you need not fear being alone again, you're not really ever alone, you always keep yourself company – enjoy your mind and the things it comes up with.

Redefining the 'Good' – Transcending Perfection

What is good, or good enough, for you? Redefining the 'good' in your life to be realistic, constructive, and free from extreme perfectionism is inherently compassionate and self-responsive. In times where your negative inner critic comes back to challenge you, you can be sure that having a healthy working attitude towards what is good and excellent will prevent its irrational conclusions from bamboozling you into believing it's negativity.

In the end, the real living being that we are is actually bigger and more accomplished than the tiny toxic stream of pitiable non-existential words that the inner critic is so desperately trying to get you to believe in. If you choose to have a goal that is worthwhile for you to pursue, then it really doesn't matter what the voice says, you can rise above it – "..we can become bigger than the [inner] critic..." [1]

Embracing Imperfection

A positive mindset is characterized by *progress*, and not by perfection. The danger of aiming for an unrealistic standard of perfection is that you come to expect perfection in yourself and in others. This can often feel like a crushing burden of insufferable superiority by the people around you. It will also put you under crushing pressure to live up to your own unrealistic high standards in every situation. If you expect perfection in this way, you will be laying the foundations for your negative self-talk to creep back into your life.

It is common for perfectionists to constantly strive to satisfy everyone around them and keep everyone happy. But, when you have an argument with someone as it inevitably will if you carry such suffocatingly high standards of perfection for yourself, then you are likely to fall into rumination over the argumentative conversation and keep replaying it in your mind. Replaying those negative highly emotionally charged conversations in your mind is essentially replaying negativity. To stop this negative self-talk and rumination from ever appearing all that need be done is to redefine the 'good' and move away from perfection as an ideal – stop trying to be perfect, you can't please everyone if you do that, least of all yourself.

Refrain from Comparison with others

Perfectionists are often a bit guilty of comparing themselves to others. If you engage in this type of comparison you are simply inviting your negative self-critic in to have a depression party in your inner mental spaces. Refrain from comparing yourself to others, rather just be present in the present moment and move between things and activities that you find personal joy in doing. One amazing capacity that the mind has is to find other people who are better off than you in some way. Instead of enjoying their success in that particular area and admiring it, perfectionists who are in the habit of comparing themselves with others will often judge themselves as deficient – which is an irrational negative judgment. Simply stop all comparisons with others, you'll always find people better or worse off than you are, and this can falsely inflate, or deflate and devalue your own sense of equilibrium, happiness, and self-worth.

Rather than comparing yourself with others to feel good or terrible, perfect or imperfect, it is far more beneficial and constructive to cultivate a sense of gratitude for what you do have and the things you are good at doing. Celebrating the tiny things and your own clear strengths and current good circumstances are one way to transcend the trap of striving for perfection. Remember that being kind and compassionate to oneself is not about adding anything to yourself because you feel you are lacking something, it is rather recognizing that which you are and realizing that that is more than enough.

So, being your best friend and transcending imperfection is basically about:

- Acknowledging what you have
- Cultivating and feeling gratitude for what you have
- Refraining from comparing oneself to others
- Working with what you have an authentic grounded starting point based on gratitude.

The above four points really are the secret recipe for preventing NST from ever returning in a meaningful way.

OTHER POWERFUL TECHNIQUES THAT WORK TO PREVENT NST FROM RETURNING

Remain Vigilant to Black and White Thinking (Polarization)

As I mentioned in Chapter 1, black and white thinking (also sometimes called polarization or 'all or nothing thinking) is the tendency to ignore progress and negatively assume failure based on not allowing grey areas, or middle ground, to exist in our cognitive evaluations. One good example is seeing yourself as a terrible person undeserving of any success or love just because you lose your temper once. That one slip of your anger and now you label yourself as completely unkind and flawed.

Black and white thinking also extends to our judgments of others. If people can only be all good or all bad, then when they happen to have a bad day and they may offend you you might see them as horrible bad people despite the long history of friendship or cordial behavior that had gone before. The truth is situations and people are never easily labeled into a neat conceptual box of either black and white. Black and white thinking is really a failure of imagination or an immature cognitive judgment because it exhibits a lack of being able to accommodate mixed and seemingly anachronous states simultaneously.

People are not complete saints, nor are they complete sinners. People are simply human beings. Human beings are complex, interesting, and remarkable wonders of nature - filled with paradox and inconsistencies.

Black and white thinking is very unrealistic, it does not account for the flux and dynamism inherent in life – things and people are changing and shifting all the time along with their life events and experiences.

You must remain vigilant and catch any instances of black and white thinking as they happen. Black and white thinking is often a type of thinking linked to underlying ideas of perfection. "If it isn't perfect it's unacceptable, flawed, a disaster". Preventing yourself from falling into extreme dualistic points of view will help prevent your negativity from resurfacing and clouding your judgments.

Practice Mindfulness & Meditation – Cultivating Gratitude Directly

Practicing meditation and visualizing your good points helps with every single aspect related to remaining positive. Meditation trains the mind to focus attention and awareness in an undistracted fashion. This means that it is an indispensable way to get better at being aware of your internal self-talk.

Practicing specific guided meditations that help you to acknowledge your positive qualities will also help you to generate self-love and compassion – a key component of preventing NST from ever returning. Meditation reduces stress, helps create detachment and distance from your internal thoughts and emotions, calms the body and mind, prevents unhealthy rumination on regrets and mistakes, and helps cultivate gratitude and self-compassion. Acknowledging your strengths and good points allows you to have a stable sense of self that can draw upon reserves of courage to face challenges and difficulties – gather the resources and energy to move forward.

Take a look at the guided visualization outlined on the next page...

A Simple Visualization to Focus on Your Good Qualities

Find a comfortable place to sit. Sit comfortably in a manner that is easy and supportive for your body. Make sure there aren't too many distractions and loud noises. Close your eyes and begin to focus on your breath moving in and out of your nose and lungs. Maintain your awareness of your breath for a count of 10.

Once your mind has settled somewhat and you are in tune with your body and breath, bring your mind's attention to a memory of a recent activity you have done, or some recent event that you were involved in that you feel good about yourself for.

Make sure to choose something simple and small and good in your eyes. Perhaps it was being kind and friendly to the sales assistant at your local supermarket or store. Perhaps you secretly washed all of your colleagues' cups at work without them realizing or acknowledging it. Perhaps you feel good about managing to wake up at dawn this morning and enjoyed the sounds of birds as you drank your morning coffee quietly in the kitchen. Perhaps you fully listened to someone who was having a bad day. Whatever you choose, make sure that you feel proud of yourself, that you were being a great version of yourself, that you liked what you did and you feel good about remembering it.

An alternative to remembering a recent behavior is to think of some good quality you feel proud of yourself for having. Perhaps you like the fact that you are patient when standing in long queues? Perhaps you enjoy being good at something or have some skill you admire in yourself. If so, then imagine yourself doing something with that quality or skill – make sure that you feel pleased and warm towards yourself when you summon an image of yourself using this skill or having this quality.

If you simply cannot think of anything positive because your NST is currently dominating your inner states, then simply acknowledge that you are actually sitting where you are, engaging in meditation to do something great for yourself. This means that at the very least you are actually being kind and constructive and compassionate to yourself because you are doing something to improve your inner dialogue and tame your mind. This means that you are determined to love yourself, find yourself, and you have your own best interests at heart – no small thing at all, you can be proud of that without conceit; celebrate and rejoice in the represent effort you have made and the progress that got you to sit and meditate.

Once you have your image in your mind, feel the sensations that arise from feeling proud or good about yourself in your body. Where are they, abide in the comfort of your own gratitude and self-acceptance – abide within the simple truth that you are capable of experiencing happiness, that you have qualities that you admire, and that you are abiding right here, right now, as yourself - nothing needs to be added to recognize that you can positively experience yourself.

Stay relaxed and drift for a time in the sensation of gratitude and self-care. Then when it begins to fade and your mind begins to wander bring attention back to the breath and count 10 in breaths to close the meditation gradually. Once you reach the count of ten, open your eyes, and slowly get up and resume your daily activities.

Don't be discouraged if you find it difficult to maintain focus during your visualization. It is quite normal for your mind to wander and get distracted – it just shows you how busy your mind is from moment to moment - Discovering that fact can be quite revealing. If you ever feel agitated, distracted, or uncomfortable you can bring your attention back to your breathing and count five in-breaths and then re-summon your memory of a deed you are proud of or a skill you are grateful for and proud of having.

FINAL THOUGHTS ON PREVENTING NST FOR GOOD

In addition to all the above, following a healthy lifestyle, eating properly, sleeping properly, reducing stress, and keeping yourself mindful from moment to moment is also tremendously positive support that will benefit all your endeavors going forward. If you put all of the advice in this chapter into practice, then by and by you will come to forget that your inner voice was anything other than the best friend that it currently is.

Having learned to challenge and change your negative self-talk, then extending your activities forward into practicing self-compassion, mindfulness, and gratitude you will have drastically reduced your risks of ever allowing your old NST to return.

LEAVE A 1-CLICK REVIEW!

Overall rating

✓ Submitted | Clear

⭐ ⭐ ⭐ ⭐ ⭐

Add a photo or video

Shoppers find images and videos more helpful than text alone.

Add a headline

What's most important to know?

Write your review

What did you like or dislike? What did you use this product for?

I would be incredibly thankful if you could just take 60 seconds to write a brief review on Amazon, even if it's just a few sentences.

Click Here to leave a quick review

REFERENCES

1. WHAT DID YOU SAY?!

1. https://advice.shinetext.com/articles/how-to-spot-and-swap-the-4-types-of-negative-self-talk/ accessed 09/2020
2. https://www.psychologytoday.com/us/basics/self-talk accessed 09/2020
3. https://www.mayoclinic.org/healthy-lifestyle/stress-management/in-depth/positive-thinking/art-20043950 accessed 09/2020
4. https://www.mayoclinic.org/healthy-lifestyle/stress-management/in-depth/positive-thinking/art-20043950 accessed 09/2020
5. https://advice.theshineapp.com/articles/feeling-stuck-open-the-door-to-new-possibilities/?utm_source=Shine&utm_medium=Blog accessed 09/2020
6. http://advice.shinetext.com/articles/stuck-in-negative-thinking-heres-what-to-do/?utm_source=Shine&utm_medium=Blog accessed 09/2020
7. https://advice.theshineapp.com/articles/feeling-stuck-open-the-door-to-new-possibilities/?utm_source=Shine&utm_medium=Blog accessed 09/2020
8. https://advice.theshineapp.com/articles/kindness-isnt-just-fluff-its-an-act-of-self-care/?utm_source=Shine&utm_medium=Blog accessed 09/2020

2. KNOW THE STAKES

1. Bressert, S. (2020) The Impact of Stress; available online at https://psychcentral.com/lib/the-impact-of-stress/ accessed 09/2020.

2. https://psytherapy.co.uk/the-dangers-of-negative-self-talk/
3. https://psytherapy.co.uk/the-dangers-of-negative-self-talk/
4. https://www.goodtherapy.org/learn-about-therapy/issues/self-criticism
5. https://www.verywellmind.com/negative-self-talk-and-how-it-affects-us-4161304#:~:text=Basically%2C%20negative%20-self%2Dtalk%20is,in%20yourself%20to%20do%20so accessed 09/2020
6. Kinderman P, Schwannauer M, Pontin E, Tai S. Psychological Processes Mediate the Impact of Familial Risk, Social Circumstances and Life Events on Mental Health. *PLoS ONE*. 2013;8(10):e76564. doi:10.1371/journal.pone.0076564
7. https://www.goodtherapy.org/learn-about-therapy/issues/self-criticism
8. Fiske A, Wetherell JL, Gatz M. Depression in Older Adults. *Annu Rev Clin Psychol.* 2009;5:363-389. doi:10.1146/annurev.clinpsy.032408.153621
9. Cheng, H., & Furnham, A. (2004). Perceived parental rearing style, self-esteem and self-criticism as predictors of happiness. *Journal of Happiness Studies, 5*, 1-21.
10. Dinger, U., Barrett, M.S., Zimmermann, J., Schauenburg, H., Wright, A.G.C., Renner, F., Zilcha-Mano, S., & Barber, J.P. (2014). Interpersonal problems, dependency, and self-criticism in major depressive disorder. *Journal of Clinical Psychology, 71*(1), 93-104
11. Yamaguchi, A., & Kim, M. (2013). Effects of Self-Criticism and Its Relationship with Depression Across Cultures. *International Journal of Psychological Studies, 5*(1), 1-10
12. Joeng, J.R., Turner, S.L. (2015). Mediators between self-criticism and depression: Fear of compassion, self-compassion, and importance to others. *Journal of Counseling Psychology, 62*(3), 453-463
13. Kopala-Sibley, D.C., Zuroff, D.C., Russell, J.J., & Moskowitz, D.S. (2013). Understanding heterogeneity in social anxiety disorder: Dependency and self-criticism moderate fear responses to interpersonal cues. *British Journal of Clinical Psychology, 53*(2), 141-156
14. https://www.goodtherapy.org/learn-about-therapy/issues/self-criticism

15. Donnellan, M. Brent, et al. "Low self-esteem is related to aggression, antisocial behavior, and delinquency." *Psychological science* 16.4 (2005): 328-335.
16. Hardy, James, Ross Roberts, and Lew Hardy. "Awareness and motivation to change negative self-talk." The Sport Psychologist 23.4 (2009): 435-450. https://www.researchgate.net/publication/278026499_Awareness_and_Motivation_to_Change_Negative_Self-Talk#pf10 (accessed 09/2020)
17. Hardy, James, Ross Roberts, and Lew Hardy. "Awareness and motivation to change negative self-talk." The Sport Psychologist 23.4 (2009): 435-450. https://www.researchgate.net/publication/278026499_Awareness_and_Motivation_to_Change_Negative_Self-Talk#pf10 (accessed 09/2020)
18. Hardy, James, Ross Roberts, and Lew Hardy. "Awareness and motivation to change negative self-talk." The Sport Psychologist 23.4 (2009): 435-450. https://www.researchgate.net/publication/278026499_Awareness_and_Motivation_to_Change_Negative_Self-Talk#pf10 (accessed 09/2020)
19. Walter N, Nikoleizig L, Alfermann D. Effects of Self-Talk Training on Competitive Anxiety, Self-Efficacy, Volitional Skills, and Performance: An Intervention Study with Junior Sub-Elite Athletes. *Sports (Basel)*. 2019;7(6):148. doi:10.3390/sports7060148
20. Tod D, Hardy J, Oliver E. Effects of Self-Talk: A Systematic Review. *J Sport Exerc Psychol*. 2011;33(5):666-687. doi:10.1123/jsep.33.5.666
21. *Molecules Of Emotion: The Science Between Mind-Body Medicine* Scribner (1999), ISBN 0-684-84634-9
22. https://brainspeak.com/how-negative-self-talk-sabotages-your-health-happiness/
23. Sutin, Angelina R., and Antonio Terracciano. "Body weight misperception in adolescence and incident obesity in young adulthood." *Psychological science* 26.4 (2015): 507-511.
24. Goodhart, Darlene E. "Some psychological effects associated with positive and negative thinking about stressful event outcomes: Was

Pollyanna right?." *Journal of personality and social psychology* 48.1 (1985): 216.
25. Ibid.
26. https://www.elitedaily.com/life/negative-thoughts-yourself/981879 accessed 09/2020
27. Ibid.

5. DETHRONING THE TYRANT

1. https://www.psychologytoday.com/us/basics/self-talk#how-to-change-your-self-talk
2. https://www.psychologytoday.com/us/basics/self-talk#how-to-change-your-self-talk
3. https://www.verywellmind.com/negative-self-talk-and-how-it-affects-us-4161304#:~:text=Basically%2C%20negative%20-self%2Dtalk%20is,in%20yourself%20to%20do%20so
4. https://www.lifehack.org/835487/negative-self-talk
5. https://www.insightforwellbeing.co.uk/meditation-leeds/47/Articles/Mastering-the-Inner-Critic.html

6. FROM TYRANT TO FRIEND

1. https://nickwignall.com/negative-self-talk/
2. https://nickwignall.com/how-to-start-a-mindfulness-practice/
3. https://www.verywellmind.com/negative-self-talk-and-how-it-affects-us-4161304#:~:text=Basically%2C%20negative%20-self%2Dtalk%20is,in%20yourself%20to%20do%20so
4. https://insighttimer.com/lindahall/guided-meditations/being-with-feelings-and-sensations
5. https://nickwignall.com/cognitive-restructuring/
6. https://www.insightforwellbeing.co.uk/meditation-leeds/47/Articles/Mastering-the-Inner-Critic.html
7. https://www.elitedaily.com/life/negative-thoughts-yourself/981879

7. THE CULTIVATION OF KINDNESS

1. https://www.psychologytoday.com/gb/blog/nurturing-self-compassion/201703/how-cultivate-more-self-compassion
2. https://www.health.harvard.edu/mental-health/4-ways-to-boost-your-self-compassion
3. https://tinybuddha.com/blog/10-ways-practice-self-compassion

8. A BRIGHT FUTURE

1. https://www.healthline.com/health/rethink-bc-negative-self-talk#Prevent:-Keep-it-from-coming-back accessed 09/2020

Printed in Great Britain
by Amazon